"From a dangerous and uncertain life in wartime Vietnam, to his escape on a leaky, crowded boat threatened by pirates, to a year in a Malaysian refugee camp, to tiny Erwin Tennessee, Larry La has become one of Washington's finest restaurateurs. In this delightful "only in America" story, you will meet dozens of Larry's most devoted customers - presidents, senators, judges, generals, ambassadors - all who love Chinese food and Larry La."

— **David Tatel**, Judge, US Court of Appeals for the D.C. Circuit (Ret.)

"I've known Larry La for over two decades, meeting him first at community events in the D.C. area, dining at his restaurant with my young children, and then having the profound honor of awarding him recognition as a "Distinguished American by Choice" when I was director of US Citizenship and Immigration Services. Larry's life story exemplifies what it really means that the US is a "nation of immigrants" and the immense loss of human potential that will result from dishonoring that legacy."

— **Leon Rodriguez**, Former Director of U.S. Citizenship and Immigration Services

"What's better than great food and deep friendship? You get both with Larry La and the hospitality is unending. He never stops working and charming everyone he meets, high and low, VIP or humble. No one better embodies the immigrant story or the eternal values of all strong families, resilient communities, and strong nations. This book tells all his secrets! Learn from them!"

— **Jim Cooper**, Former U.S. representative for Tennessee's 5$^{th}$ congressional district

"Larry Trung La is an American success story. He and his family were Vietnamese boat people who were settled in a small town, Erwin, East Tennessee where my family came into contact with him. We became friends. I witnessed his rise as a "gopher" at a railroad company, through college and then a successful restaurant owner. He is a testament to family, friends and the American spirit."

— **Thomas J. Seeley, Jr.,** Circuit Court Judge with the State of Tennessee(Ret.)

"SQUARE MOON will grab your attention and heart on page one and keep both until its conclusion. Larry La's book is two intertwined stories. The first is about his extended family's perilous journey to America from war-torn Vietnam in the late-1970s. The second is about how perseverance, family, and entrepreneurship enabled Larry to build an extraordinarily successful restaurant business in the Washington, DC area. This business provided Larry with a platform to play a role in people-to-people diplomacy in the nation's capital. At this moment in our national history, this book reminds us how central the immigrant story is to America's past, current, and future successes."

— **David M. Lampton**, is Professor Emeritus of China Studies at Johns Hopkins University—SAIS, former President of the National Committee on U.S.-China Relations, and former Chairman of The Asia Foundation

# Square
# MOON

# Square
# MOON

One Man's Journey
From War-Torn Vietnam to
D.C.'s Hottest Kitchens

*By*

**LARRY TRUNG LA**

**QUADERER**
MEDIA GROUP

Quaderer Media Group
175 Varick Street
New York, NY 10014

Square Moon

Copyright © 2024 by Larry Trung La
All rights reserved.

No part of this book may be reproduced, stored in a retrieval system, or transmitted in any form or by any means – electronic, mechanical, photocopying, recording, or otherwise – without prior written permission from the publisher, except by a reviewer who may quote brief passages in a review.

Published by Quaderer Media Group
175 Varick Street, New York NY 10014
www.quaderer.com

First Edition: November, 2024
ISBN: 979-8-9916659-1-9

Library of Congress Control Number: 2024951384

The information in this book is based on the author's experience and research. While the author and publisher have made every effort to ensure that the information in this book is accurate, they cannot assume responsibility for errors or omissions, nor are they liable for any loss or damage arising from reliance on the information contained herein.

For information about special discounts for bulk purchases, please contact info@quaderer.com.

Printed in the United States of America

*For my beloved parents*

# FOREWORD

## By Joie Chen
### Asian American Broadcast Journalist

It's almost impossible to miss the connection. A genial, humble "Southerner" of 'everyman' roots, who somehow repeatedly finds himself in the midst of world events, sitting side-by-side with world leaders—advising them as only someone with his unique perspective can.

The only thing that separates him from the fictional character "*Forrest Gump*" is Larry La's intellect.

Even the adage Forrest's mother teaches him applies to Larry's story: life is like a box of chocolates—you never know what you're going to get.

Certainly, no one anticipated his life as a merchant's son in southern Vietnam would be upended by civil conflict (which he reminds us, is how the people of his country remember what we call the "Vietnam War.") Or that his whole family would be driven to take the cataclysmic risk of fleeing by rickety boat across the waters of the South China Sea.

I recall in one of our first conversations, now more than 20 years ago, Larry matter-of-factly telling me, "Yeah, I'm one of what they call the 'boat people.'" Like most Americans, I knew something of the 800,000 people who fled Vietnam in the harrowing time after the fall of Saigon, but only in the most abstract way. I had seen the photos and news coverage of refugees clinging to makeshift rafts and overcrowded, not-very-seaworthy craft. I had read that as many as half of the boat people never made it to the 'safety' of primitive refugee camps along the Gulf of Thailand.

But I had never met one before—and wouldn't have imagined someone who had survived such an ordeal could speak so calmly and casually about it.

That's Larry, though. A man with no pretense. Fifty years after the end of the war, he writes this volume not to memorialize or commemorate or even politicize the conflict. Instead, his book takes a straightforward approach to chronicling the gunfights and battles that blocked his way home from school, or tying himself to the captain's quarters to keep from being pitched overboard while he slept, or gambling that the damaged boat could make it to shore without capsizing or being intercepted.

He tells me he is simply lucky. Lucky that the overcrowded boat bearing nearly 300 desperate people finally reached shore. Lucky that his family was able to find basic shelter in a simple and very crowded Malaysian refugee camp. Lucky that his English skills were noticed by "Madame Ann," who gave him the opportunity to work with NGO leaders which allowed him to see outside the confines of the camp.

And ultimately, to leave it for an exotic location called "Erwin, Tennessee." A small community in far East Tennessee, it sits in a valley near the North Carolina border. As late as the 1990s, the entire Asian population of the state of Tennessee was less than one percent; even today, the latest census counts only 11 people of Asian descent living in the town of Erwin.

It couldn't have been easy to be an outsider in such an insular community. But his persistent determination to win over skeptics, coupled with a constant smile and a cheerful greeting—no matter how unwelcome— would help him win a place in the community in the end. "They would find out we are people just like them. Attitude is very important."

Larry's approach to any discrimination he faced is a reminder of his family's values and their influence on his life. "One's behavior," he tells me, "changes others' perceptions of you. Everywhere there are people who discriminate. How you overcome that is by how you behave in a new environment."

He refers often and thoughtfully to the example set by his father, who came to Vietnam as a Chinese immigrant. An outsider in a country where he didn't know the language, Larry's father modeled an inclusive approach. In a break with culture, he made a practice of dining with his employees— unusual for the owner of the business, especially in the Asian culture.

In his own business, Larry has followed the same path. Step into his upscale Mei-Wah restaurant just over the Maryland line from D.C., you'll find the same team members who have worked with him for decades— going all the way back to the early days of the well-known City Lights of China restaurant at Dupont Circle. These people are a family, he says, who trust him as much as he trusts them.

When I first arrived in DC in the early 2000s as a correspondent for CBS News, my new colleagues repeatedly asked if I knew Larry or had been to Mei-Wah "yet." Each one of them announced their 'must-have' dish from the restaurant—I remember frequent calls for "orangey beef" and "steamed dumplings." It wasn't much of a journey to pick up take-out; the CBS Washington bureau at 2020 M Street sits almost catty-corner to the original Mei-Wah in West End. My own son, then barely two-years-old remembers regular visits for "rice and 'one-time' (won ton) soup" served by Uncle Bob—then the jovial front door host.

But I admit I was at first a little annoyed to think that my new colleagues assumed I must know this Larry La guy; just because we both trace our family roots to China doesn't mean we "all know each other!" But I quickly learned I had misread the situation entirely.

It was actually that everyone, from political leaders to business chiefs to network anchors to street-level couriers and everyone in between, everyone in Washington seemed to know Larry and everyone ate at Mei-Wah. And he has the receipts to prove it: what became known as the "ME-Wah" wall was an honored tradition in DC.

Photos of Larry with all of those 'everyones' lined the walls of the restaurant. It was an honor to have your picture with Larry put up on the wall. Colleagues would come back after lunch and say, "I sat by your picture today." Every once in a while, some photographs would be moved to less favored walls to make room for a new member of Congress, or Cabinet secretary or news anchor or even some beyond-the-Beltway celebrities (even the Rolling Stones!) The sharp-eyed would take notice and demand, "Where's MY picture?"

Larry didn't post those pictures just because he was star-struck. He collected photos like friends, showing all were important and welcome, no matter their status or political party. "The restaurant business is very tough," he says. "If you don't like to deal with people, you just can't do it. We take care of everybody; we must be friends to everybody no matter their politics."

And in Washington, that's often a difficult line to walk.

In recent years, Larry— the biggest non-journalist news junkie I've ever known—has watched the reports of a spike in anti-Asian violence with great concern. People need to be educated about immigrants, he says. And newcomers can help; "Asians in particular, how you approach people, open yourself to them can make a difference." And so, there he is, always impeccably dressed in suit and tie, and always, always smiling and welcoming, making a difference by simply being there.

As you read Larry's story, his remarkable journey from a happy childhood through the violence of civil war, from the edge of safety in a refugee camp to the great unknown of East Tennessee, from life as a railroad worker to master of multiple successful, upscale restaurants in the nation's capital, from takeout deliveryman to the First Lady's box at the State of the Union, I hope you'll consider why he's telling his story now.

I asked if it's because of the coming 50th anniversary of the fall of Saigon. No, he says. That's just coincidence. Or perhaps it's because a number of school districts across the country are adding Asian-American studies to their curriculum—maybe this could be a text? Not really, he says.

This is Larry's story for his children and now, his beloved grandchildren. And all of us he welcomes as family. So that we may understand that, despite all he has been through, why Larry La believes he is truly a lucky man, and how he made his own luck.

# PROLOGUE

What's a guy like me doing in Small Town, Tennessee? It's sometime in the late 1970s, and the war in Vietnam, and all the troubles its tragic conclusion brought about, are turning into memories from an increasingly distant past.

That was the idea.

It's why my father handed over so many gold pieces to the owner of a rickety fishing boat that ferried my family away from my birth country's southern shore. It's why we crossed dangerous waters on what proved to be a deadly pilgrimage to a Malaysian refugee camp, where we toiled in prison-like conditions for more than a year before finally gaining passage to America on the basis of political asylum.

It's why my family came to a place where our faces looked like no one else's — to forget, as best we could, and start anew. The poem inscribed on the base of the Statue of Liberty reads: "Give me your tired, your poor, your huddled masses yearning to breathe free, the wretched refuse of your teeming shore," so we could've done much worse.

Most everyone here in Erwin is kind and has been welcoming. I'm so grateful to so many of them for helping my family and I get acclimated to our chosen homeland. But some of them have a penchant for reminding me of my status as perhaps the town's most unique citizen.

It's 11 p.m. Employed by the Clinchfield Railroad company as a laborer at the diesel shop, waiting outside the facility for the third shift crew to check in, my affable coworker looks up at the night sky. Mr. William Rogers is in his 60s; I'm in my 20s. Like almost all of his neighbors — as well as his neighbors' parents, and even their parents' parents — he's lived in Erwin his entire life. Contemplating our collective existence I suppose, he asks me, "Back in Vietnam, do you have the same moon that we have here?"

Always a bit of a jokester, immediately I say, "No, ours is square."

After answering his unexpected question, I would assume that we both would have a good laugh together. Instead, Bill nods his head and says, "OK, so your moon is square."

"Bill, I'm kidding with you," I say, guilt washing over me for having taken advantage of his innocent naiveté.

"What do you mean?" he asks. "Didn't you just tell me that your moon in Vietnam is square?"

I smile and just say, "Our moon is the same as yours."

It's hardly the only thing I have in common with the people of the United States of America.

# CHAPTER 1

All of my boyhood remembrances are of war. Back then, we simply called it "the Civil War." Today, with on-the-nose elaborateness, the government of my home country calls it "the Resistance War Against America to Save the Nation." However, the people of my *chosen* land, where I've now lived for nearly 45 years, refer to the conflict as "the Vietnam War."

Whatever its name, my family and I experienced the horrors that come with any war every single day. I was born and grew up in the Trà Vinh province of South Vietnam, part of the Mekong Delta region, close to the southern tip of the country. My parents were Chinese immigrants to Vietnam in the 1930s when China was in turmoil during its own Civil War. I was the middle child of nine, with three of my siblings being boys and five of them girls. My mother gracefully took on all the responsibilities of a typical homemaker. Fortunately, my father was a successful businessman. He sold herbal medicines, as a retailer and wholesaler, out of his own market that was attached to the front of our four-floor house. Part of the reason I think his business did so well was because he treated his workers wonderfully. When he ate a meal every day, his male staff dined with him inside our home, and the women who worked for him ate alongside my mother, too.

Unlike many others in Vietnam, my family and I never lacked in everyday needs. It was outside our home where problems resided.

We heard explosions and gunfire, both loudly and faintly, on a constant basis. In a strange way, those sounds became very welcome music to our ears. We had a saying, and it was true: "If you hear explosions, that means you are alive."

On my walks home from my elementary school, it was a normal occurrence to see dead bodies in the street. We wouldn't run away from them or anything. My classmates and I sometimes approached the cadavers to get a closer look and determine if they were from the Army of the South or if they were Communist guerillas, which was given away by their clothing. They could have been our friends; they could have been our enemies. It was impossible to know in a country divided in two.

The Army of the Republic of Vietnam, fighting for the democratic South, was supported by the United States, both financially and in terms of manpower, weapons, vehicles and supplies. Together, they were fighting the Viet Cong supported by North Vietnam, the Communist half of the country, who called themselves "the Liberation Army in the South." Whatever their name, in addition to striking targets and forces of the South, Northern soldiers and operators regularly infiltrated the South's government and army, making it a particularly challenging war to fight.

When I was 13 years old, my father sent me to Saigon, the capital of South Vietnam, to attend middle school. I remained in Saigon until we left Vietnam by boat in 1978.

In 1968, I was about 300 miles away from my boyhood home, living with family friends. One night I stood atop the building in which I lived with my host family and watched the Tet Offensive play out violently, destructively across the city below us. "Tet" is the Vietnamese New Year. Everyone was convinced there would be a ceasefire as people throughout the country, in both the North and South, celebrated. In

Saigon, we did for three days, but then the Viet Cong grabbed hold of the arms they'd smuggled into the city and began their sneak attack. We saw helicopters launch rockets, with flames shooting out both ends of turrets, and we tracked the paths of rockets all the way to their targets, watching them explode. It was just like in the movies, except real life.

For some reason, it didn't feel all that dangerous. We were used to it, so desensitized to the chaos, that we just carried on without an exceptional amount of consideration to what was happening — though there were plenty of moments when the fighting was so close we had to go hide.

At the end of high school, like everyone else my age in Vietnam, I had to pass a national examination. It was conducted at the same time across the country for three consecutive days. If you failed this exam, you lost the chance to apply for college and you had to join the military immediately and fight in the ongoing war. Failure meant immediate conscription into the military. If you passed the test, it still did not guarantee your acceptance into college. Each university had its own entrance exam, and if you didn't pass any of them, then you had to join the military immediately and fight in the ongoing war. I took entrance exams for three different universities. Luckily, I passed all of them so I could choose the university I liked the most: the South Vietnam National School of Commerce (Quốc Gia Thương Mại) located in Saigon. I wanted to honor my father by following his footsteps into entrepreneurship.

I would regularly travel home to Trà Vinh by bus, a trip that normally took about four hours. But sometimes the bus ran into fighting.

One time, the driver stopped in the middle of the road, turned around and said, "Everybody get off the bus!" I exited on the right-hand side of the vehicle, and there were South Vietnamese soldiers right in front of me shooting at men in the distance ahead of us. Bullet shells were falling at my feet. They would've scalded my hand if I tried to pick them up. Soon they pushed the Viet Cong back into the jungle. We jumped back on board the bus and soldiers from the unit accompanied us on our way. That trip from Saigon to Trà Vinh took the entire day. There were other bus trips where the riders and I stayed overnight in some random village to wait out a battle.

Another time, my fellow students and I were forced to leave school during class. In early April of 1975, a South Vietnamese lieutenant pilot who was actually a North Vietnamese sympathizer, diverted his assigned mission and instead bombed the Presidential Palace in the middle of Saigon. We were only allowed back to school when the fighting calmed.

Armed coup attempts, or at least the threat of them, were also a regular occurrence. All of the South was unstable before the Fall of Saigon. When I watched the riot at the United States Capitol Building on January 6, 2021, it reminded me of what it was like in Vietnam as a young man. This time is different from those coups d'état that happened in Vietnam before. This time, it is very personal to me and my family. As the mob breached the Capitol, my daughter Alisa, a close aide to House Speaker Nancy Pelosi, and her colleagues barricaded themselves in a room in the Speaker's office suite hiding in the dark as the rioters ransacked it, hearing those awful haunting noises. Her life could be in danger if those insurrectionists opened the door. This was the first time I saw something horrible happen in my 45 years living in this great country.

*\*\**

After years of negotiations, a cease-fire agreement by the Communist forces of North Vietnam and the South Vietnam Army along with the United States was signed in 1973. The Paris Peace Accords meant an end to the fighting, but it also meant the withdrawal of U.S forces. Everyone in South Vietnam knew it was just a matter of time before the army from the North invaded again.

By April 1975, after capturing a string of provinces on their way to Saigon, the Viet Cong reached the capital city. By that time, I was a freshman in college. On the 30th day of that month, the Southern forces and government of the Republic surrendered. The announcement was broadcast on television and over the radio. The North called it "the Liberation of the South Vietnamese" and the "unification" of the country. The South called it "the day they *lost* the country." Whatever its name, Saigon erupted into anarchy.

I saw on TV, tanks of the Northern forces knocking down the Presidential Palace gate, and soldiers emerging on the building's roof to raise the red/blue flag with a golden star in the center — the flag of the so-called National Liberation Front of South Vietnam. That was the official end of the Republic of South Vietnam.

People feared what Northern soldiers would do to those associated with "the resistance movement" of the South once they took total control of the city. Everyone tied to the government or the U.S., even loosely, wanted out right away. Many left, by any means necessary: boat, helicopter, plane, it didn't matter. The U.S. Navy helped people escape, shipping them to refugee camps in nearby U.S. Territories like Guam.

Ordinary citizens like myself were scared, too. What might the Northerners do to a person they even *suspected* was part of the fight against them? What was keeping them from believing any of us could have been involved? The answer was: not a whole lot. So just about everyone, including myself, wondered what to do next.

But most of my classmates and teachers realized that we didn't actually know where to go. If we did, there would've been the question of how to get there. So, we figured we just had to — quite anxiously — wait and see what happened.

One week after the fall of Saigon, the Northern Army's general who took over Saigon, Trần Văn Trà, ordered all of the students to report to their school and march toward the Presidential Palace, now occupied by his army. We did what we were told, and it seemed like a million people were in the streets. We heard someone talking over a loudspeaker, but we were so far away from the speaker we couldn't see who it was. Regardless, we were told the new government was that *of* the people, and it would take good care of the people. They said we shouldn't worry about our safety. After that, my classmates and I felt a little bit better about our chances of survival.

Then, in September 1975, the new government instituted the official currency in South Vietnam. It was changed to the "liberation dong," one of which was worth 500 in the old Southern dong. There were mad dashes by locals to get the new currency because their money was useless. The chaos didn't stop there.

Government officials soon showed up to the school and ordered us to work. We worked on farms, tended to roads by clearing trees and debris and did other municipal jobs. The new rulers believed that the more people were focused on labor, the quicker they could rebuild the country. Fortunately, the forced labor we were prescribed wasn't exactly a death sentence. We put in a full day's work, and then we camped out in the jungle, sleeping in tents. We were provided meals. My classmates and I treated it like we were on a school field trip.

Our new leaders told us that the country had to become self-sufficient and, again, that Communism was for the people. We also had to learn about Communist theory and prove that we understood and accepted it by passing different exams. It was a widespread attempt at brainwashing throughout the South.

After two years of reorganizing the government and society in the region, the Communist officials reopened the schools. However, instead of re-attending business school, which was considered capitalist and totally abolished, my classmates and I were forced to take classes in mechanical engineering. The thinking behind this was that we would be trained to build things to help the country function better and thrive. We certainly wouldn't be able to go into business for ourselves. We had a sense that if we didn't go along with their wishes, we'd be subject to hard labor. It didn't seem worthwhile to resist.

# CHAPTER 2

In October 1978, my family decided we had to leave the country. Like many people, we weren't very happy with life under the Communist regime.

We yearned for freedom.

Slowly but surely, the government began taking over individual businesses, just like what had happened in China after their country's own Communist revolution, something my father was quite familiar with. He was petrified over losing his business, and with it his home, especially because he was ethnic-Chinese.

Dad was also concerned that if we didn't leave Vietnam soon, we might miss our chance to ever get out. My oldest brother, Jiadong Luo, went to China to live with my grandparents in 1949, just as the Communist takeover was reaching its conclusion. Like me, he was ordered to work for the government on farms during the Cultural Revolution era. Even though he was approaching his 34th birthday and I was 21, we'd never met in person. My father desperately wanted to go see his parents again and be reunited with his first born, but Dad rightly presumed that the democratic South Vietnamese government wouldn't take too kindly to one of its citizens visiting a Communist nation while it was at war with one. (He took a huge risk once visiting China through Hong Kong.)

The government in Vietnam had taken over food distribution, and shortages began. Another big problem in the South even before the Fall of Saigon was inflation. Whether your money was in a bank or under a mattress at home it was decreasing in value every single day. Smartly, whenever my father made money he would immediately buy things the family needed. He also purchased small amounts of gold, and sometimes he would exchange his cash for American dollars. All these measures made his financial wealth impervious to local inflation.

We secretly listened to the news of the world on radio, tuning into the British Broadcast Corporation and the Voice of America. Though this was against the law, we learned from the broadcasts that people were leaving Vietnam by boat, eventually settling in countries in Western Europe and Scandinavia, New Zealand and Australia, as well as Canada and the United States.

To do this ourselves, first we had to secure a place on a boat by paying its owner and a local government official. In a way, I was very lucky. Unlike many of my fellow Vietnamese citizens, my parents were born in China, and the Communist government willingly turned a blind eye to people of Chinese descent leaving the country. There was a growing conflict between Vietnam and China, which eventually led to the brief Sino-Vietnamese War in early 1979. So, as long as my family handed over a certain amount of gold to the right government representative, we were free to go. From there, we'd travel to a nearby country like Thailand, Indonesia, Malaysia or the Philippines, and find passage elsewhere. We weren't completely sure where we'd end up. The only thing we knew at that time was to get out of Vietnam, with the motto in mind: "Rather Dead than Red."

The going rate for passage out of Vietnam was 11 ounces of gold for an adult and half of that for a child. It was an official policy as a matter of fact. The government knew that many of its citizens were hoarding gold because of the increasing inflation, and its officials were more than happy to collect some of it back. They got quite a bit from the La family.

On my father's bill were my two parents, seven of my siblings, the wife of one of my younger brothers, and my older sister's husband and their three children — a grand total of 14 people, broken down by 11 adults and three kids. One ounce of gold was worth about $200 in 1978, which meant my father had to spend nearly $28,000 just to ensure we'd get on a boat, with no guarantee of a successful migration anywhere.

As I write this in 2024, that amount translates to more than $130,000.

\* \* \*

My family and I arrived at the Seagate of Binh Dai, in the Mekong Delta city of Bến Tre, and boarded a boat that was about 20 feet wide and 60 feet long. It was a fishing boat that had been converted to transport people, with a second-level deck and a tin-roof added on the top to cover passengers on the deck. Ultimately, that roof wasn't very good at deflecting rain. The luggage was stored on top of the cabin where the boat's owners stayed and the captain and co-captain operated the vessel.

It took a long time for everyone to get on board. By the time all the passengers had stepped off the pier, the boat was jam-packed with people. All the young men, like me, were in the bottom of the boat, below deck, encased in the wooden hull. The young kids, older men and women were above us. We just sat there still like sardines. Some of us stood. There was no room for the passengers to lie down.

Before the boat took off, some people in the bottom found big cracks in two support beams, which may have just developed under the weight of so many people on deck. We feared it might collapse anytime. Everyone was yelling to alarm the captain and the boat owner.

They came down to the hull, looked at the beams and assessed that the boat had to be repaired before taking off.

Off the boat we went. We had to wait two days to try our trip again. But that wasn't going to demotivate us. At that time, we learned that our house in Tra Vinh was already confiscated by the Communist government. If we stayed, we would have become homeless.

When the repairs to the support beams were complete, the passengers all got back on board. Shortly after we left the pier and traveled about six nautical miles, heading toward international waters, the boat suddenly struck a coral reef. There was a loud, heavy impact. Everyone shook; many people fell down. For a moment, I didn't think we would survive. A crack in the hull opened up and water started coming inside.

Thankfully, we had two pumps that we used to get the water out, but the boat was stuck in the coral. The captain of the boat decided to throw luggage overboard to lighten the load and help free the hull. We decided not to go back to shore for repairs, fearing some problems with the Communist government. Instead, we relied on the two pumps to continue working. Fortunately, they did, and we avoided a fate at the bottom of the Pacific Ocean. If we had ended up there, we wouldn't have been alone. It was estimated that half of the boats that left Vietnam during the years between 1977 to 1981 never made it to their destinations.

\* \* \*

There was one bathroom on the boat that everyone took turns using. The only food was bread.

After about a day and a half at sea, most of the men working on the boat — who weren't really sailors, just family of the boat's owner — got seasick. Because I remained healthy, I actually took a job on the boat, replacing one of the seasick workers above deck, in the open air, which was much more pleasant in some ways. One of my duties, though, was washing the bags people used to catch their vomit when they threw up. A positive that came from so many people getting sick was that we didn't run out of food. Not too many people wanted to eat in the first place. Water was essential of course, and distributing good old H2O to the passengers was another one of my jobs.

At night I slept on top of the captain's cabin where the remaining luggage was stored. I tied my arm and my leg to heavy pieces of luggage because, if I rolled over off the top of the boat in my sleep, I'd be gone for good. It would have been too dangerous to stop the boat and rescue someone who went overboard, which the captain of the boat had announced at the start of our voyage.

My responsibilities on the boat had one big drawback. Every time I saw my parents, they would ask me, "So when are we going to land?" They thought my connection to the captain meant I'd have some greater insight into what was going on, but I didn't have an answer for them. The captain didn't tell me anything. Like them, all I saw was the sky and deep, dark blue water.

We endured high waves and heavy rains at times. By the third day of the journey, I heard someone crying. One of the elderly passengers died. He wasn't feeling well when he got on the boat and his health continued to deteriorate. He was unable to handle the poor conditions. After he passed away, there wasn't much else to do other than wrap his body up in a bag and toss him into the ocean. As a volunteer sailor, I was one of the four people that held onto one of his limbs as we threw his body overboard. It was all a shock to us and difficult to deal with. But the boat kept moving, and so did we.

After five days at sea, the captain suddenly had a very grave look on his face. Until that point, he always seemed rather optimistic, but that morning he was unsure if we'd make it safely to the next harbor. It turned out that the captain used to be in charge of merchant ships that frequently traveled from Vietnam to East Malaysia. Those trips took four or five days, but our trip was taking longer. We were on a smaller boat that had a smaller engine, with many people on board, plus their luggage. He hadn't considered those variables in his planning and grew discouraged.

Another concern — for everyone — was that we would be targeted by Thai pirates. We'd heard stories of their aggression on the radio, robbing passengers at gunpoint of money and valuables. Fortunately, no pirates saw us while we were at sea, but the longer we were out there, the more tense everyone got.

Finally, on the eighth day in the ocean, we came across a fishing boat operated by a crew of Chinese Malaysian who spoke Mandarin. Because most of us were Chinese Vietnamese, we asked them in Mandarin for directions to a place we could settle temporarily. The fishermen pointed us in the right direction.

Finally, after nine days in the Pacific Ocean, we landed at Borneo Island, Kuching, the capital city of the East Malaysian state of Sarawak.

We were stopped by the Malaysian police and navy, but were allowed to temporarily stay ashore. We were so happy to have survived the ocean. However, there was still a long way to go before we reached our respective finish lines and settled in new countries for good. Plenty of uncertainty remained.

\* \* \*

For three days we stuck around the area where we'd landed. Many of us pitched in to help the local fishermen during the day, and at night we slept outside on the beach. The navy provided us with meals.

The Malaysian government had established a refugee camp for Vietnamese refugees, and we were soon sent there. It was located in the middle of the jungle with no habitants around us. Saying the refugee camp was like a jail would be a bit too harsh, candidly. But there *were* barbed wire fences all around us, and we weren't allowed to leave the grounds. Some refugees had been there for a few months while they figured out a way to get to their final destination. When our bus arrived at the camp, many of them came to greet us, excited to see if there were people from Vietnam that they knew. We were excited to see them, too.

There were about 800 or 900 people at the camp, organized in blocks of housing for about 100 each. My family and I lived on H Block, the last row of "homes." They were small wooden hovels with a stove and bunks that were outfitted with mosquito nets so we didn't get bitten in our sleep. In the middle of each block there were pieces of firewood, enough for about 50 people living on either side.

During the day there wasn't much to do. People would go to the river behind the camp where everyone bathed. They carried water back to the camp to wash their clothes, too. But a lot of the time, because the river tended to be muddy, the cleanest water we had access to was rainwater. Even if it rained in the middle of the night we'd wake up and go outside to take a shower. We also stored rainwater in big containers that we'd use for cooking. The Malaysian Red Crescent also supplied us with drinking water once a week.

I later learned about conditions at other refugee camps in West Malaysia that were much worse. There was one in West Malaysia, on Pulau Bidong Island, where as many as 40,000 Vietnamese stayed at a time. It was very crowded and unsettled. But at our camp in Sarawak, we were given food by the Malaysian Red Crescent — that country's version of the Red Cross — and there were English language classes and church masses. It was difficult, but just like in Vietnam during the fighting, then on the boat on the way to Malaysia, my family and I adjusted.

Because so many people came and went, the Malaysian Red Crescent always needed new folks to help them out. I was asked to work in the warehouse where they stored food and supplies, primarily because I spoke Mandarin and a little bit of English. My job was to receive and distribute food to everyone in the camp. I kept track of stock, what came in and what was distributed to the refugees. We had rice, canned food and some fresh food, too, which varied day by day. After a while working in this position, I got to know every family on the island. I could automatically determine what they needed after a given amount of time passed between their visits to the warehouse.

I remember helping one particular Vietnamese family of four that was struck by greater hardship than mine had been. The family's patriarch had unfortunately contracted leprosy and had to be treated at a facility away from the camp. Word got around the camp that his wife and two children had been exposed to the disease, and they had trouble finding a block where they could live. I understood that leprosy was not easily transmitted and noncommunicable. I arranged for that family to stay at the small church that was only used on Sunday morning. I even brought their share of food and supplies to them every day.

Then, after about three months at the camp, the family gained sponsorship to Norway. Through my work with the Malaysian Red Crescent, I met Mrs. Amar Jeet Katar Singh, an officer with the organization. Everyone addressed her "Madame Ann." She spoke wonderful Cantonese, which I learned when I was studying in Saigon, and we got along very well, growing close over those difficult months. She was blown away by my ability to recall the names of people in the various families in the camp. "Wow, you're like a computer," she said to me one time.

I helped her with some paperwork as she processed information about the campers. Along with her, I traveled to the leprosy treatment facility where that struggling family's father was staying to tell him he and his family were on their way to Scandinavia. I delivered the news in Vietnamese. When I spoke, he looked extremely surprised.

"You're the first Malaysian who's spoken to me in Vietnamese in three months!" he said. Apparently, he didn't speak any Chinese, English or any other language that anyone in the facility could speak.

"Oh, I'm not Malaysian," I said. "I'm a refugee from Vietnam just like you."

He was so appreciative to learn that he could leave the facility and travel with his family to a new home in Norway. I was happy they were able to leave, too — maybe even a little envious.

My multilingual status also meant I could help members of the United Nations' Refugee Agency, the UNHCR, as they logged names of the people who came through the camps and helped them find a place to permanently settle. I wound up becoming kind of an important member of the camp community, in all honesty. It was through this work that I found out 292 people, including the old man who died, were aboard the ship that transported my family and me to Malaysia from Vietnam.

\* \* \*

People from the American embassy came to our camp on a frequent basis to interview refugees and determine if they were seeking political asylum and whether they would be good citizens of the United States.

But at first, my family and I thought we would eventually wind up in Australia. We figured that, because Australia was known for its big farms, and Vietnam was a country with a rich agricultural history, its government would consider us a natural fit. Though people from the Australian embassy didn't come to our camp as frequently as those from the American one, after six months in the camp waiting, some Australian delegates interviewed us.

The Australian officials accepted my parents and I, as well as my four siblings who were not married, but not my three other siblings who were married. My two older sisters and my younger brother, each of whom were betrothed, were considered by the Australian delegates to be in separate families. It seemed for a few minutes like our six-month stay in an East Malaysian refugee camp was about to come to an end, and, as you can imagine, we were thrilled. But after learning that some of my siblings and their spouses and kids wouldn't come with us, we were disappointed. We weren't going to leave the refugee camp without them.

The next day, however, delegates from the American embassy approved passage for my married siblings. When the Australian embassy got wind of that, they denied the rest of my family's admission to their country. I'd also been helping those Aussie delegates with some of their work as an interpreter, too. Because I was familiar with them, I boldly asked why they took back their promise of our entry. They said, "Well, we don't want you to settle in Australia and then later on you sponsor everyone else in your family to come join you. We have a big continent, but it's mostly desert, and we don't want to take *that* many people."

Once again, we were stuck. But I'd gotten to know the representative of the United Nations High Commissioner for Refugees in Asia and the Pacific, Mr. Rene van Rooyen, pretty well. He asked me if my family and I wanted to go to the United States of America. I said, "Yes, why not?" He took me to see the American Embassy delegates and the matter was settled quickly: My whole family, immediate and extended, were all going to the USA. We were sworn in right away.

I'm glad it turned out that way. The United States has always been — and will always be — the best place on earth for refugees and immigrants. The tapestry of America has been woven by immigrants and refugees, all of us adding our own unique imprint.

My family and I were ready to make our own mark.

*Family picture in front of family store, Tra Vinh*

*National School of Commerce building 1975*

*Larry La in charge of the food distribution in the refugee camp*

*In front of my childhood house in Tra Vinh 2024*

*Escaped boat docked at the river behind the camp*

*Block H, My 'house' in the refugee camp*

*At Kuching airport leaving the refugee camp, with Madame Ann in 1979*

# CHAPTER 3

There was still one more step to take before my family could settle in the U.S. My family and I required an American sponsor before we could leave the refugee camp.

Fortunately for me, while we waited, Madame Ann frequently took me to her office so that I could help her with paperwork in a more ideal setting than that of a Malaysian refugee camp. I was one of the few folks in the camp — maybe the only one while I was there — who left on a regular basis. Her office was located in the downtown section of Kuching. So often in life, when you are dealing with misfortune, incredible, positive things can happen. This helps balance out the memories, as long as you choose to hold on to them all.

One time I went to Madame Ann's office it happened to be the day of the Conference of Rulers. That's when the Malaysian monarchy elects among itself a new head of state called the Yang di-Pertuan Agong. Essentially, because Malaysia has nine states, each ruled by a king, this is the crowning of a new King of Kings. Each of the nine kings rolled through Kuching in a nice car waving to the crowd in a huge celebration that happened once every five years. The year I was there, Madame Ann and I left her office for lunch, but when we noticed a mob of people collecting next to the street, Madame Ann realized what was on the way.

We waited for the procession to go through the street. I bet none of those nine kings knew they were waving to a Vietnamese refugee when they passed by me. I would venture to guess I was the only one among all refugees in Malaysia that got to see all the Sultans of Malaysia.

\*\*\*

When I wasn't working back at the camp, to kill time while we waited for sponsorship to the U.S., my family and I studied English. I helped them and other refugees as best I could, especially when it came to spelling and grammar. (My accent when speaking English was pretty pronounced, and it still is, but I always wrote well in the language!)

My younger brother, Ngoc La, the one who was married, left the camp first with his wife. He got passage to Greenville, Tennessee, sponsored by a church. One of my married sisters, Hue-Anh, and her family ended up in Greenville, too, also sponsored by a church. My other married sister, Lien-Anh, went to Maryland after she was sponsored by her husband's family.

It was hard to find a sponsor for the seven people in my family that remained in Malaysia. But eventually we did. It was the First Baptist Church of Tennessee, in the town of Erwin. We had no idea where Tennessee was, nor Erwin. We'd heard of Los Angeles, San Francisco, Chicago and New York, famous places like that, but not Erwin, Tennessee. It didn't matter, though. It was the good news we'd been waiting so long to hear. We were on our way to America, and we were so happy. It was perfect because the rest of us would be close to my brother and sister in Greenville, Tennessee.

Madame Ann delivered the news to my family at the camp. Like she'd done so many times before, she brought a list of people and families who'd gained sponsorship, which I would often read out to attentive camp residents, but mine was never on it. "Hey Ann," I told her one time, "when is my family's name going to be on this?" It finally was.

However, before we could actually travel to the U.S., we had to spend some time in what they called a transition camp, where they examined the health of refugees. If you were healthy enough, you were on the next flight out. The transition camp was in the capital city of Malaysia, Kuala Lumpur. We had to stay there for a few more weeks, but we eventually got through our examination and received permission to go to the U.S.

We took a flight to Hong Kong, where we stayed overnight. We then flew to Hawaii, our port of entry, where we had our paperwork checked by immigration agents who were there waiting for us. It was quite an emotional moment. We were excited, of course, but we were also quite nervous, unsure if this step in the journey would go smoothly. We thought maybe there would be some error that would keep us from going forward. But, thank goodness, the officers let us pass.

From there, we flew to Los Angeles, California, and then to Atlanta, Georgia, for another connecting flight to Charlotte, North Carolina, before we ultimately ended up at the Tri-Cities Airport in Blountville, Tennessee. It was November 29, 1979. When my family and I looked out the window during the plane's descent, our mouths were agape. There was snow on the mountaintops below us and on the ground of the airport. When we deboarded the plane, we had to walk on the snow to the terminal, excited to step on the white stuff for the first time in our lives. The only other time we'd even seen snow in our lives, I think, was when we watched *Doctor Zhivago*, the epic movie that took place in Russia.

We were dressed for tropical weather, not for ski slopes. But I remember the first thing Mrs. Ruth Johnson from the First Baptist Church of Tennessee did the second I met her in the terminal was put her coat over me. My whole family then piled into the church's van and we were driven 40 more miles to Erwin, Tennessee. The Keesecker family, also members of the church, owned an apartment in the downtown area of Erwin. They'd donated it to the church's cause and let us live free.

Finally, our nearly 14-month pilgrimage to freedom was complete.

# CHAPTER 4

My family members and I never locked the door to our apartment. There was nothing for anyone to steal anyway, but, regardless, it was a safe small town and we were in a place owned by very generous and caring people. While we adjusted to the time difference, we slept during the day, and people from the church filled our refrigerator with food, which we would eat at night. You can imagine how much food we consumed after so long in a refugee camp! It was like a miracle to have so much food refilled when we woke up. We ate like pigs, to be sure, but there was no shame in it.

We certainly weren't judged by anyone. A member of the First Baptist Church who was also Mayor of Erwin, Dr. L.D. "Dale" Mullins, was the driving force behind our sponsorship. That made me very proud, and I made sure to tell people I met in town all about it. Part of the reason I think Dr. Mullins wanted to help people like us was because he and his wife were missionaries in Indonesia during the 1970s. They were familiar with Asian culture and Mrs. Mullins actually came to our apartment and cooked us some delicious food that reminded us of home, it was that authentic-tasting. The Mullins family also invited us over to their home where we watched television for the first time on a color set.

Another story of generosity in Erwin: I had to make sure that I mailed the letters I'd collected from fellow refugees back in Malaysia who had relatives already living in the U.S. But I didn't have any money for stamps, which cost 15 cents each back then. Fortunately, Mrs. Ruth Johnson gave me $20, which was enough to cover the postage for all of the letters. I was so happy I helped those people — with the assistance of Ruth.

* * *

It took my family and I nearly a week to get used to the time change. When we did, we started to meet more people, from the church and out and about in town, which was home to roughly four or five thousand people. There was one main thoroughfare, a couple banks, a McDonald's, a high school, a theater — what you picture when you think of a small American town.

We lived in the residence owned by the Keeseckers for six months, and then moved into government housing.

My siblings, who were still teenagers, went to high school, which was a difficult transition for them. Their English language skills were not well developed. Some people in the town did offer to tutor them in English during after school hours, which was very nice of them.

Because I was older than 18, I went to work. After the Comprehensive Employment and Training Act was enacted by Congress in 1973, there were programs set up across the country to help people get jobs in public service. I was one of its beneficiaries. Through that program, I got a minimum-wage job for $3.10 an hour, working at the high school in Erwin, helping teachers with many of their tasks. I also functioned as a math tutor. (I spoke the best English out of anyone in my family, but it wasn't good enough at that point to help the kids with much else besides mathematics.) My older sister, Thu-Anh, also got a job at a garment factory sewing clothes, and with the money we earned, and the help of the church, we were able to support the family. We never applied for food stamps or similar government aid like that at any point.

I also chose an American English name for myself, thinking my Vietnamese name, "Trung," would be a little difficult for people in Erwin to say. I landed on "Jones," which sounded a bit like "Trung." The locals went with it and some of them even called me "Jonesy," which I enjoyed.

* * *

Dr. Mullins came to my aid once again, helping me to get an even better job with the Clinchfield Railroad Company, a regional railroad that mainly shipped coal out of West Virginia mines into Virginia and North Carolina for further export. In Erwin, Clinchfield was a big company that was important to the local economy, and obtaining a job there was not easy. But before I knew it, thanks to Dr. Mullins, there I was with an interviewer, fielding a job offer for janitorial work with a pay rate of $7.25 an hour, more than double the minimum wage at the time. I was shocked at the amount. I didn't expect to get more than minimum wage — which I was already making, and was happy with. When the shock wore off, I was excited.

The assistant general manager of the railroad office, Mr. Bob Sam, brought me around and introduced me to the other people who worked there. Some of them would greet me by saying, "What you say?" I was confused, and just thought to myself, "I didn't say anything yet, I just got here." But after a couple days, I asked some of my coworkers what the greeting meant and learned it was a common way to say "hello" in Erwin. Then I adjusted, and in response said things like, "Oh, not much. How about you?"

At first, I worked as a janitor and errand boy, a "gopher" in the company's main headquarters. I cleaned the offices, the bathrooms, mopped the floor, anything they needed. At 5 p.m., the other workers would leave, and I would bring the mail they left behind to the post office. After a while I got to know workers there, too, and eventually they'd let me in through the back door after normal business hours. Mr. Fred Davis, who processed the mail and sometimes worked at the customer service window, became a particularly close friend.

I worked very hard, keeping the offices tidy and making the floors shine brightly. I also made the water fountain look like a mirror, and people complimented me on a job well done.

Upon being hired by the Clinchfield Railroad, employees were automatically unionized. Early in my tenure with the company, I was "kicked" many times, moving from one job to the other, because I didn't have seniority. I was transferred from the headquarters to work in the company's warehouse. I was trained to drive the forklift and load and unload heavy palettes to and from the 18-wheeler trucks. Another "kick" saw me transferred to the diesel shop where I cleaned locomotives arriving for refueling and maintenance. During the second shift, from 3:00 p.m. to 11 p.m., I also carried the "knuckles," or couplers, which were used for joining rail cars with locomotives. Those knuckles are pretty heavy! I only weighed about 115 pounds at that time, but I think I handled them well overall, once I got used to the task.

The Clinchfield Railroad Company played a vital role in my family and I receiving our immigration papers. The company's general counsel, who went on to become a judge, Tom Seeley, wrote a letter on behalf of us to the U.S. Senator Jim Sasser. Senator Sasser's office asked the Immigration office in Memphis, Tennessee, to process us quickly. My family of 14 had to drive 10 hours, in two cars, from Erwin to Memphis, so we could get the paperwork done. Staying at a hotel was too expensive, but because of that letter from Senator Sasser we didn't need to worry about that. Everything was finished in less than two hours. We turned around and drove another 10 hours back.

* * *

Over the course of the next year or two, my family began to move away from Erwin. My younger brother, Dinh, graduated from high school and was accepted to the University of Maryland. When my younger sisters, To-Anh and Ngoc-Anh, finished high school, To-Anh moved to Ohio and Ngoc-Anh to California. And my beloved mother and father, who sacrificed so much to make sure I got the best education I could and live in the country with the most opportunities, moved to Miami, Florida. They liked the more familiar warm weather down there. It was also too difficult for them to live in a small town like Erwin, with limited English-speaking skills and no other Asian people around. In Miami, there was at least a small community of Asian migrants and Asian Americans, and there were more business opportunities for them as well.

I remained in Erwin, working my union job at the Clinchfield Railroad. Unfortunately, my lack of seniority led to the most severe "kick" yet — out of the company completely. A year after I was hired, I was laid off because a more senior member of the union needed to take over my position. The coal miners union went on strike, which meant less business for the railroad, and that I had to go on unemployment.

Mr. Tom Seeley called me into his office. He began to tell me that the reason I was being let go wasn't because of my race. I quickly told him that I understood how unions worked from studying American history, particularly the Industrial Revolution, which gave rise to unions. He was surprised by my knowledge, but also relieved that he didn't have to explain it too deeply to calm me down. I just accepted that that was how the union worked.

Knowing that I needed a job, my brother-in-law, Henry, said that I could move to Silver Spring, Maryland, and work in the restaurant where he was employed. The place was in a Marriott Hotel and called Koni Kai, a Hawaiian-Chinese fusion restaurant in Bethesda. It sounded good to me: my first restaurant job.

I moved in with my sister and brother-in-law and worked at Koni Kai as a food runner for a month. I enjoyed the work, and was happy to have it at that point in my life. But my focus was on my education and eventually establishing a career for myself, not necessarily in the hospitality industry. So, when I got a call from Mr. Bob Sam, Assistant Manager at Clinchfield Railroad, asking me if I was ready to go back to work for him in Erwin, I said, "Yes sir!" The coal mine was back up and running, business was better for the train company, and my position reopened. I was happy to be back.

Living in a small town like Erwin, I understood that people are skeptical when meeting a total stranger from the other side of the globe. When I wasn't working, I would go around town, shopping. I'd say hello to people on the street and stick out my hand for a shake. If they shook it back that was great; if they didn't, that was OK, too. I'd just say, "Have a nice day, sir" or "ma'am." I understood they didn't know who I was. If they wanted to be my friend, we could be friends. If they didn't, I had to go on living anyway.

But doing this helped me get to know many people around town. They started to notice that there was a new person here, who was also one-of-a-kind: the only Asian American in Erwin. They sometimes looked at me almost like I was a panda.

One person thought she should take advantage of my presence in town — in a good way. Mrs. Ruth Johnson, from the First Baptist Church, had a sister, Ila Nielsen, who was a middle school teacher. Mrs. Nielsen, also a member of the church, asked if she could bring her students to visit me at my home one evening after school. She kept asking me whether I wanted to know the reason for the visit. I said, "No, I do not have to know the reason." After she asked again, I told her to go ahead and tell me why. She gave me the reason: "The kids just want to see what a Chinese person looks like."

I happily agreed. When they arrived and I started speaking to them in English, they were so surprised. I explained to them that I learned the language back in Vietnam and had continued to study it at the camp in Malaysia and in Erwin.

Having already acquired Southern hospitality, I asked them whether they wanted to have some "Chinese Coke" — which was just Coca Cola served by a Chinese man born in Vietnam. All the kids raised their hands, so everyone had a cup of so-called "Chinese Coke." They loved it. I kept joking that everything in the house was Chinese, even the tap water.

I experienced many other moments of warmth in Erwin, like when I applied for my first credit card. My application was denied, not because I had bad credit, but because I had *no* credit. The chairman of the Erwin National Bank, one of only two banks in town, heard about my problem. He invited me to his office to explain the credit rating in my new country. (Only in a place like Erwin could I meet a bank chairman and have him tutor me in person on finance!) He told me that in the U.S. you had to borrow money in order to build up your credit history. He offered me a loan of $3,000 even though I did not need that money; however, by paying that loan back regularly — and early — I established a favorable credit history. I was soon able to get my first credit card with a $500 credit line.

When I was working for minimum wage, there was a young doctor in town named Robert Quinn, Jr., who also helped me and my family. Dr. Quinn was not a member of the First Baptist Church, which had sponsored my family, but he was my mother's doctor and because we did not own a car, offered the service of a house call, like in the old days. He stopped by to check out my mom on his way home from his office.

Wanting to help me and my family any way he could, Dr. Quinn also offered me a job helping him lay bricks in his home's backyard. I didn't know anything about laying bricks, but figured I'd work together with him and get the hang of it. He picked me up on a Saturday morning and we went to work. At noon I had lunch with Dr. Quinn and his family, then we worked for a few more hours. He took me home and paid me for one day of work.

A few years later, Dr. Quinn moved back to Nashville, where he was from. We invited him and his family to our apartment to have a Vietnamese dinner and to say farewell. After he left, our church's treasurer told me that an anonymous donor left $3,000 with the church to give to our family. The donor made the church promise not to tell us who the money was from. As much as we needed money at the time, I insisted that people from our culture could not accept such an offering without knowing who the kind donor was. Eventually, the church's treasurer buckled and exposed the donor as Dr. Quinn. What a generous gentleman!

\* \* \*

I did run into some people during my time in Erwin who were not so nice, who did worse things than refuse to shake my hand on the street. There were a couple guys at work who'd call me names. If I addressed a coworker, sometimes they would pretend I wasn't talking to them. Other people would respond to me in harsh tones, saying things like, "I don't understand you."

Once when that happened, I stood proudly and said to the guy, "Look, I'm trying to speak your language. I'm not speaking Chinese or Vietnamese to you. Don't you think you can maybe try a little harder to understand me?" His eyes widened. Then I said, "If you can't understand my English, that's your problem, and if I can't understand your English, that's your problem, too. So, either way it is your problem."

"Why's that?" he said, still looking surprised.

"Let me explain," I said. "You speak your mother tongue to a foreigner, so don't you think you could do that in a way that makes sense to foreigners? And if a foreigner is trying to speak your language, don't you think you should try to understand that person? Therefore, either way it's your problem."

He nodded his head and said, "You're right." From then on, we were friends. He didn't pick on me anymore.

Soon, someone at the local weekly newspaper, the *Erwin Record*, the only weekly newspaper in town, decided to interview me. When they published the article, it was on the front page with a picture of me smiling, like I always did when I walked the streets. The article told the story of my life up to that point, and I tried to give the impression that my intention was to be an upstanding citizen of the United States. I told the interviewer that if Erwin's residents were a little skeptical of me, I understood, but I also assured readers that I was happily adapting to American life and wanted to be part of the town.

I bought a bunch of copies for my family. They were so proud. And people around Erwin began treating me even better than they had before. In fact, many of them offered to help me in various ways, including helping me with my English, which continued to improve and was crucial to me functioning as the best citizen I could be.

*\*\*\**

While working at the railroad full-time, I also attended East Tennessee State University, 15 miles north of Erwin, in Johnson City, Tennessee. For the *third time* in my life, I was a college freshman. The first time was in 1974 under the South Vietnam government; the second time was in 1976 under the Communist regime. I'm pretty sure I was one of the few people in the world who's thrice been a college freshman. I thought to myself that I had to work hard to finish my college degree.

Mrs. Martha Stromberg, one of the members of the First Baptist Church, also a graduate student at ETSU, introduced me to the school. But the reason I was able to actually attend classes there was the generosity of Mr. Lloyd Bell. He was in charge of admissions for international students. I had a meeting with him and explained that I'd finished high school in Vietnam, and that I'd begun collegiate studies elsewhere — on *two* occasions. But because I was a refugee, I didn't have any diplomas or transcripts. I hadn't taken the SAT, the ACT, or even the TOFEL exam. But Mr. Bell was well-informed about the education system in South Vietnam, and he said he could tell by talking to me that I was as educated as I said I was.

I was admitted to ETSU without any documents or tests.

At first, I went to school part-time because I couldn't afford more classes. (On my janitorial salary I was still helping to support my family.)

But after a while I applied for the PELL grant, named after Senator Clairborne Pell of Rhode Island. To qualify for it, I had to go to school full-time, which meant taking at least 12 credits a semester — a heavy school workload on top of my position with the railroad. But it was the best way for me to ensure I finally earned a degree, so I had to do it. The PELL grant helped pay for my tuition and my books for the first two years. Then, when the Clinchfield Railroad merged with other railroad companies to form the CSX Transportation company, the new organization offered tuition reimbursement, which I also took advantage of. (Someone told me, to my amazement, that I was the only worker at the Clinchfield Division of the company to do so at that time.) I just had to maintain a grade average of "C" or above and I did. I always aimed at an "A" anyway, so "C" or above was not hard for me at all.

It was my father who taught me to have such a strong work ethic and it's also because of him that I have an aptitude for business. At ETSU I was able to engage with my entrepreneurial spirit for the first significant time in America. Using that first credit card of mine, which had a $500 limit, I purchased computer floppy disks in bulk from a catalog. I then sold them individually to some of my classmates for a profit.

It was 1981 when I began coursework at ETSU. Ronald Reagan had just been elected President of the United States of America. As part of his platform, he said the country's defense was a top priority, so I thought a career in computer science would be useful. That's what I majored in, and I enjoyed it. But it was very difficult to study computer science back then because the mainframe computers we used were so massive. There were these humongous terminals in the computer lab that the students had to take turns using, and we had limited time with which we could finish our assignments. (To think that, today, in my pocket, I carry around a computer that's much stronger and faster than those I worked on during college is very amusing.)

But I did my best, often staying after class to speak to the professors. I did that because sometimes I couldn't understand what they were saying during class, due to my language barrier. I didn't want to waste the time of the other students during class by interrupting with repeated requests for clarification. All the teachers there were very patient with me, helping me after class whenever I asked for some extra assistance, which I appreciate to this day.

I always carried with me a small tape recorder and a portable dictionary, which were key tools in my effort to master the English language. I also realized that if I sat in the front of the classroom I could hear the teachers better and understand them better as well. I also looked at the mouths of the teachers as they spoke, so I could imitate how they enunciated. To improve my English even further, I went to the English Department and asked if they had a speech therapy course. They said they didn't, but to make up for it they asked a graduate student who was working in the office to help me with my speaking twice a week, one-on-one. In America, speaking English well is very important, so I made it a priority. I even practiced pronunciation loudly while taking showers.

* * *

Though I experienced a few challenges at work in my initial months there, my race was not otherwise too problematic for people around me, in Erwin or at school at East Tennessee State University. That wasn't the case for a couple of my classmates, though. There were some African American students in my computer science program who were all from another state, living on campus. When I told them I lived in Erwin, they were shocked.

"They let you live there?" one of them asked.

It was strange and upsetting to think that Erwin had the kind of reputation where people of color believed they couldn't go there. Well, in the 20th century, Erwin was considered a sundown town. The people of Erwin embraced me. I went to the local Kiwanis Club and a book club and talked about life in Vietnam. I did the same in front of a history class at Erwin High School when they were studying the Vietnam War. (I held up a recent cover of *TIME* magazine that featured Mr. Lech Walesa, leader of the Polish Solidarity Movement against authoritarian Communist rule. Under a photo of his face read the caption: "He Dares to Hope." None of the students in front of me understood exactly what that meant. They'd been born in a free country and could hope for anything. Coming from Vietnam, I knew firsthand that that wasn't the case in places like Poland.)

In Erwin I even joked about race with white friends of mine, including Fred Davis, from the post office. He said to me one day, "Hey Jonesy, you know, we consider you to be a honky."

"What's 'honky'?" I asked him. "They never taught me that word in school."

Fred laughed and said, "That's not the kind of word they teach people in schools." Then, he explained to me what it meant, and I laughed. It was also kind of a compliment, that they would consider me to be one of them in a way.

"You can call me 'Honky Davis,'" Fred said kiddingly. Every once in a while I did and we'd laugh about it.

Years later, after keeping in touch with many people from Erwin, even after moving elsewhere, I got word from town that Fred had passed away. I called his wife, Barbara, to give her my condolences.

She picked up the phone and I said, "Hello, I'm Jones La, an old friend of Honky Davis." Barbara laughed so hard. I later heard from Fred's daughter, Marcella, that that night the family was all together, reminiscing, and she told everyone what I'd called him and they all laughed, too.

* * *

After my second year in college at ETSU, I changed my major. I realized I didn't want to spend my entire professional life sitting in front of a screen. From then on, I studied business, my original focus back in Vietnam. With the railroad, sometimes I had to work the third shift, the so-called "graveyard shift, from 11:00 P.M. to 7:00 AM. After work, I went straight to school attending classes, then took a good nap at the school library before driving home. I could have finished my degree sooner if I didn't have to maintain a full-time job, but I still completed coursework for a business administration bachelor's degree, with a focus on finance, in four and a half years. I also had enough credits in computer science to have it featured on my diploma as a minor, and I graduated with honors — something I'm very proud of.

In addition to my parents and other family members, Bob Sam and Tom Sealey from the CSX Transportation company's Clinchfield Division actually attended my graduation ceremony in 1984. They wanted to see the only person from the Clinchfield Division who received tuition reimbursement get his diploma. It was so nice to have that support from them. I also made them proud that I graduated with honors.

I had a similar experience in 1985 when I was awarded United States citizenship. I studied for a long time for the exam, and was tutored by a retired college professor named Lois Hall, who I met when I spoke at the book club. Ms. Lois Hall even asked me to recite the "Declaration of Independence" in front of a local Historic Society meeting.

It was so nice of her to be invested in my journey toward American citizenship — though, actually, the whole town of Erwin seemed to be invested in it, too. By then I'd been living there for more than five years and had made many friends. Because I was the only immigrant living in town, they all knew I was working toward obtaining citizenship, so I felt a lot of pressure to pass the test.

Thankfully, I did. The swearing-in ceremony was held in Greenville, where every year the court awarded citizenship to new Americans from four or five different counties in East Tennessee. In a typical year, including 1985, there were about 40 people sworn in as citizens from the entire area. They would be at the courthouse with maybe a family member or two — about a hundred people total. But the day I was sworn in the courtroom was packed, and the judge was surprised.

After the ceremony, I told the judge that the reason there were so many people in the courtroom was because I was the only immigrant in Erwin, and a lot of my friends showed up. That was a beautiful day for me.

My status led to a funny interaction when an Erwin resident originally from England sought citizenship. Their attorney, Ms. Clark, called me up and asked me about the process. I immediately showed off my level of familiarity by telling her: "Ms. Clark, I have to 'clock you' now," something I heard lawyers say to their clients, including me, many times by that point. She laughed and said, "Well, you've learned things fast!"

\* \* \*

Over time, I started noticing a pattern when I first interacted with people in America. They would ask me my name and I would say, "Jones." They often responded, "No, what is your *first* name?"

I said, "That is my first name. Don't you think I'm one of the Joneses?" It turned out that "Jones" is one of the few last names that is not popular to be a first name.

But I got tired of explaining it and thought I should change my first name. My Chinese name is Law Wen, which sounds a little bit like "Lawrence," so I went with "Larry." It was friendly and easy to remember.

I also began to miss my family after a while, and I wanted greater professional opportunities for myself than what I was finding in Erwin. I joined my parents and my older sister, Thu-Anh, in Miami, in 1986, shortly after I earned my bachelor's degree. Realizing my lifelong dream of being an entrepreneur, I opened a small Oriental grocery store after saving money for years while working at the railroad company. My parents and my sister also kicked in some capital and we all worked together there. I handled the behind-the-scenes business; they handled the customers. I also began coursework for a master's in business (MBA) at Florida International University — a degree I would never finish.

Life had other plans.

# CHAPTER 5

I'd been a bachelor my entire time in America, and I started to notice that mostly women came into the grocery store I owned. It was all moms and their (age-appropriate) daughters, many of whom were new to the country. I used to joke to my family, "If you want to find a wife in the United States, open a grocery store." That wound up being a prophecy.

I became active in the Asian-American community in Miami, helping a lot of people with immigration paperwork especially. Once again, my English-speaking skills were key. So when Diana Phuong came into the grocery store, it wasn't long after we started talking that I realized I knew her relatives, who I'd helped many times before. She was also from Vietnam. Her aunt was living in Miami and sponsored her and her family's entry into the U.S. as immigrants in 1987. Diana also worked for her aunt at her Chinese restaurant.

At first, we were friends, but Diana is a very kind person and family-oriented, which I liked and related to. I took her to see the movie *Coming To America* on our first date, which in some ways was a bit on the nose.

Our budding romantic relationship was almost sideswiped when some friends of hers asked why she was dating a guy with so little money. What gave them that impression was that I was still driving a beaten-up Mazda from the model year 1980. It had a stick shift and no air conditioning, not even a radio. I'd bought it when I *really* didn't have a lot of money back in Erwin. It cost $5,000 without any additional features, which was all I could afford with the loan from the Clinchfield Railroad credit union in 1982. She told me that her friends questioned her judgment because of the car. I just laughed. The Mazda still worked, and I prioritized other things with the cash I earned. Besides, it was nice to know Diana was with me for everything else I brought to the relationship and not just money.

* * *

Life was pretty good for me in Miami. I had my business, much of my family was close by, and I was falling in love. Diana and I got engaged not long after we met, having a party to mark the occasion with many families, friends and people we knew in the community.

Soon, my father, who'd also become a citizen in the mid-1980s, sponsored Jiadong and his family. In 1987, my brother Ngoc and I went to China for the first time to bring my brother, Jiandong, to the USA to reunite with our family I was finally able to meet my oldest brother, Jiadong, in person for the first time. We took a train from Hong Kong to Guangzhou, the Guangdong Province capital, and met my brother at the station. He had a picture of me in his wallet to make sure he recognized me. It was a heck of a moment. We embraced each other and cried together, emotional because for so long we weren't sure if we'd ever meet.

The three of us then went to the place where my father was born and grew up, DaBu, a poor town in a rural part of Guangdong Province. Then we traveled to Beijing and enjoyed ourselves in the Chinese capital, a first for all of us.

Jiadong brought his wife as well as his six-year-old son with him, who later graduated college at U.C. Davis, a terrific school, with a double major.

But a big life change came for me in 1988. I got a phone call from my brother-in-law, Henry, who was still in Maryland with my sister and his family. Henry kindly presented me with an opportunity to run a restaurant in Washington D.C. The place was called City Lights of China, and it resided in D.C.'s Dupont Circle section, located in a basement-level commercial space on Connecticut Avenue. City Lights of China had not yet been open for a year, but there was some conflict among the owners. Henry had been the manager/owner of another Chinese restaurant, in D.C.'s Chinatown, and became friends with the City Lights of China head chef. The chef's wife worked for Henry and would often go to Henry's restaurant to pick her up after his shift.

One night, he showed up and told Henry, "Well, no work for me tomorrow."

"What happened?" Henry asked.

The chef said that his partners at City Lights of China bought him out. Henry asked him why he didn't buy *them* out.

"I do not have enough money, and I cannot manage the front of the restaurant because of my limited English," the chef replied.

"I have a brother-in-law in Miami who could do that," said Henry. He knew my English was very good and that I had experience managing a business with my grocery store.

"That's great, but I don't have enough money to buy the City Lights guys out," the chef told Henry.

"Larry has money that he can use to buy into your partners' shares," my brother-in-law said.

I drove my Mazda with no air conditioning from Miami to Maryland in the hot summer, and stayed with my sister and my brother-in-law. Then, I took a couple trips through the D.C. metropolis and liked what I saw. Always an intense lover of politics, it was intoxicating to be in the nation's capital. Diana thought running the restaurant seemed like a great opportunity, so I agreed to become a junior partner and manager of City Lights of China.

When I arrived at City Lights of China in 1988, the dining room only had 55 seats and wasn't doing good business at the time. In fact, it was taking on a large amount of debt. I negotiated with the owner of the adjacent building to expand the space to hold 120 people at one time with no delivery service. I told my Chef/partner that we did not have enough chairs and tables for our daily customers, we should be able to put our food at the dining tables of our customers at their home. We then started to have delivery service, from one driver to 13 drivers by the time I sold my shares in 1998. Our carry-out and delivery services were so busy that our phone lines were constantly engaged. As soon as we hung up, the phone rang right away.

Within a few years we increased our monthly revenue from $60,000 to $300,000 and we paid down our debt. I also made sure to establish good working conditions for my employees, just like my father did for his staff back at his market in Vietnam. I think most people who've worked for me — some of whom have done so for more than 20 years — would say that the restaurant staff feels like a family. For that I'm very proud.

Diana, my then fiancée, stayed in Miami for six months while I got my feet underneath me up north. Then, we got married in Miami and relocated to Montgomery County, a northern suburb of D.C. in the great state of Maryland. We've lived there, now, for more than 35 years.

# SQUARE MOON

\* \* \*

A stroke of good fortune came shortly after I joined City Lights of China. Ms. Phyllis Richman, a highly regarded and powerful restaurant critic for the *Washington Post*, wrote a strong review of City Lights of China. She praised the decor of the dining rooms, calling them "soothing and flashy," and noting that that was "a difficult balance" to pull off. She praised the wine list and our frozen daiquiris, as well as a number of selections from the food menu.

"City Lights of China is not a restaurant to dazzle, but a restaurant to please with modestly good food and a generous spirit," she wrote. While that might not have been overwhelmingly positive, the restaurant was always intended to be humble. So, it was an accurate assessment, and a boon to our business.

Word spread around town that City Lights of China was an enjoyable place to eat, and before we knew it, we were sending orders to the White House, which at that time was home to George H.W. Bush, the 41st President of the United States. In 1989, when he announced the arrest of Panamanian General Manuel Noriega — the target of a U.S. military operation in the country he ruled as a military dictator — that made for a long evening for the press. Many of them ordered food from the restaurant for dinner and I got to know them a little bit after personally delivering their food.

Over the years, a number of White House workers became valued repeat customers, too, and an increasing number of politicians, including former Governor of Arizona Bruce Babbitt, who ran for President in 1988 and then became President Bill Clinton's Secretary of Interior in 1993 for eight years. We also served Clinton's first Chief of Staff, Mack McLarty, as well as George Stephanopoulos, a top Clinton advisor who went on to have a huge career in the media as a political analyst. Oklahoma Senator David Boren was a customer, and so were the Supreme Court Justices Sandra Day O'Connor, John Paul Stevens, as well as Antonin Scalia, who became a regular that I met many times. During that time, I also got to know Congressman Jim Cooper from Nashville, Tennessee. With the Tennessee connection, we became good friends for many decades. We value our friendship even today after he retired from Congress.

The restaurant was always crowded. There were long lines to get into the place; our reservation book was jam-packed with names on most days. But I knew who to make exceptions for. In our Capital City, some politicians who have been in D.C. a long time have big egos. Some of them assumed everyone in town knew who they were, and if they didn't, those people *should* know who they are.

Early one evening, Ohio Senator Howard Metzenbaum personally called to make a reservation for 7:30 p.m. that same night. We'd just hired a woman from China to take bookings, and when he called, I happened to be standing next to her. I heard his voice on the phone, and I heard him ask for the reservation. Then I heard my employee tell him we were booked up and couldn't provide him a table at the time he requested one. That was a big no-no for someone of his stature in Washington D.C. However, I didn't want to take over the phone call and tell him I knew who he was. If I did, I would have had to honor his request, one that could not be fulfilled. I decided to let her handle the call.

Thankfully, she did so gracefully, and Senator Metzenbaum settled for an 8 p.m. reservation. But then when it came time to write down his name, she struggled mightily. Understandably, the spelling of "Metzenbaum" was problematic for someone who was learning the English language. But when he said the table was for "Senator Metzenbaum," she actually asked him, "Is 'Senator' your first name?" If he was sitting down, I'm sure Senator Metzenbaum fell out of his chair over that one.

When Senator Metzenbaum arrived, he brought a guest: Senator Frank Lautenberg, from New Jersey. When Senator Metzenbaum was finished with his dinner, I approached him.

"How was everything this evening?" I asked.

"The food was great," he said, "but your girl gave me a hard time."

At first, I thought he meant the waitress assigned to his table. But he corrected me.

"No," he said, "the girl who took my reservation."

I apologized, gave him my business card and told him: "Senator, call me directly if you ever want to come again and I'll take care of you, personally." I wouldn't make a potential guest like him wait for a table if I could help it.

That made him very happy. It's how one must treat certain people if you work in the restaurant business in Washington D.C.

Both Senator Metzenbaum and Lautenberg became friendly regulars.

Then there was the time in 1991 when U.S. Attorney General Bill Barr came into the restaurant and had to make an urgent call to President Bush. This was before the time of smartphones, but he did have a beeper. He asked if he could use my office for privacy's sake. Without much needed consideration, I said he could, but warned him that my office was very messy. He said he didn't mind, but I still straightened up a little bit, quickly, before he made his call. (Years later, my daughter, Alisa, who worked for Nancy Pelosi when she was Speaker of the House of Representatives, was at an event when Bill Barr was again A.G. in 2019. She happened to be standing next to him and tried to start a non-political conversation. She asked if he remembered having to make a phone call to President Bush from the back of a Chinese restaurant. He actually did remember! She told him that was her father's place.)

Henry Cisneros, Bill Clinton's Secretary of Housing and Urban Development, also had to use that phone in a pinch, on one occasion. So did the acting Solicitor General, Walter Dellinger, who used the same phone in my office shortly after appearing in front of the Supreme Court on behalf of President Clinton during the Paula Jones sexual harassment lawsuit proceedings. As I understand it, the Attorney General at the time, Janet Reno, had beeped him to find out how the day in court had gone.

One might say my office phone at City Lights of China was pretty historic. Being a political junkie, I loved it.

Sometimes, though, restaurant owners can't be completely accommodating to the clientele. Another Clinton cabinet member, the former Senator from Texas, Lloyd Bentsen, who'd become Secretary of the Treasury, came to City Lights of China a couple weeks after Senator Metzenbaum did. I recognized Secretary Bentsen immediately, remembering him from the 1988 presidential campaign of Michael Dukakis, for whom he served as running mate. Secretary Bentsen famously took part in a Vice-Presidential debate against Dan Quayle, who was running at that time with Presidential candidate George H.W. Bush. Quayle was a U.S. Senator and in the debate was asked a question about his experience level in politics. He said he had as much as John F. Kennedy did before he became President. To that, Secretary Bentsen said, "Senator, I served with Jack Kennedy. I knew Jack Kennedy. Jack Kennedy was a friend of mine. Senator, you're no Jack Kennedy."

Not long after that, into the City Lights of China walked Secretary Bentsen. His wife was with him, and he asked for a table for two. He didn't have a reservation. Unfortunately, all of my tables were taken.

"I'm so sorry Senator, I don't have any tables available at the moment," I said. "It will be about 20 minutes. Is that OK with you?"

"No," he said. "I can't wait that long."

I apologized again and gave him my business card. I told him to call me ahead of time before his next visit and that I'd take care of him. I felt so bad. It was the U.S. Secretary of the Treasury, one of the most powerful people in the world!

He left and 20 minutes later he called me from his home. He addressed me by my first name, and said, "My wife and I would like to dine at home and have some of your restaurant's food. Can I send a driver to pick some up?"

Of course, I said yes, and I couldn't help but feel good about American society. If something like that happened in Vietnam or China, and I didn't sit a government official immediately, I'd be in trouble — *big* trouble. I would have had to buy a table from my customers in order to seat him and his wife. But I turned Secretary Bentsen away and he didn't have any bad feelings about it at all. In fact, he ordered from us that night and for many years afterward. I love the freedom of my adopted country. What a great feeling I have about this great nation's democracy!

* * *

Perhaps the best thing about working in the restaurant business is getting to know so many different kinds of people. That's the most rewarding return you get for all the hard work you do. And when you own a popular restaurant in Washington D.C., you get to meet people who are a very unique mix of powerful and interesting. In my case, there was Jesse Jackson; Al Franken, before he became a U.S. Senator; James

Woolsey, Director of the CIA; and John Paul Stevens, the Supreme Court Justice, to name just a few folks I interacted with at City Lights of China. There were TV journalists David Brinkley, Chris Wallace, John Martin and Bernard Shaw, as well as the big boss from the *Washington Post*, the publication's president Tom Ferguson, and his famous writers, Bob Kaiser, Bob Woodward and Ben Bradlee.

I also served many famous pop culture icons, including Chuck Berry, Natalie Cole and some notable actors like Alan Alda, Adam West and Rod Steiger. A pretty famous Senator from Tennessee, Fred Thompson, the one who acted in some Hollywood films, was also a customer of mine. He said, "Your food here is very good. You should open another place like it in Nashville where I'm from." I said to him, "Senator Thompson, maybe when you leave the Senate we can open one together. We'll call it 'Fred and Larry's.'" We both laughed and I added, "Don't worry, you won't have to work in the kitchen; just come by the place to say hello to our customers a few times a week and that'll be enough."

One of my favorite people who I met at City Lights of China was the Clinton White House Official Photographer, Ralph Alswang. Ralph would come by frequently, dining in or sometimes out. But we had many conversations and we became friends. Sometimes he came in late when the restaurant was already closed and stayed to eat with me and my employees. He's really down to earth and, like me, has a great sense of humor. We just hit it off really well. Years later, he was a guest at my daughter's wedding, where he was kind enough to also serve as the official wedding photographer.

Incredibly, my time running D.C. restaurants even gave me a chance to reconnect with people partly responsible for my passage to America and my eventual achievements in business.

In 1991, I learned from one of my customers that a man who worked for the United Nations High Commissioner for Refugees in Asia and the Pacific at the time my family and I were in the Malaysian camp had ascended to a higher position in the organization. He was about to take over the Washington D.C. office as the agency's representative in the United States. That office was located right across the street from City Lights of China. I asked if he was Dutch and they said yes.

"Hm," I said. "I bet that's the guy I know."

Two weeks later, I walked over to the office and I said hello to Mr. Rene van Rooyen, the very same Rene van Rooyen who helped my family leave the Malaysian refugee camp! He looked about the same, but he didn't recognize me at first. Back when I was in the camp, I had long hair, sandblasted skin and wore shorts. I looked quite different as a restaurant manager. But after we talked for a few minutes, I'd done enough to jog his memory.

"What are you doing with yourself now?" he asked.

I walked him over to his office's window, pointed at City Lights of China and said, "I'm a managing partner at that restaurant."

"Oh, wow!" he said. "So you're doing quite well."

From then on, City Lights of China became a refugee restaurant. Anytime the United Nations High Commissioner for Refugees had big meetings with diplomats from around the world, they were held over dinner at City Lights. Once we welcomed the High Commissioner of the entire agency, Ms. Sadako Ogata, from Geneva, Switzerland. I bet I'm the only refugee in the world — or at least from Southeast Asia — who's reunited with the actual representative of UNHCR who handled their passage to a new, safer country.

Another man who transitioned from customer to friend is a man named Mr. Mike Heller, who works in hotel design. He's been a customer of mine for more than 30 years, but there's one day in 1994 that was certainly the most memorable for him. He was at City Lights and my staff were seating a table for seven. Someone from the Ritz Carlton hotel had made the reservation, but didn't give the real name of the primary person who was coming in to eat. I was working in the back of the restaurant, and in walks Mike Heller, who was so excited he could barely put two words together. Eventually, he was able to say, "You have no idea how big of a guest you have out there right now."

"Who is it?" I said.

"Mick Jagger," replied Mike.

"Who?"

Incredulous, Mike said, "Mick Jagger! The Rolling Stone!"

"Oh, I think I've heard of the Rolling Stones, but I don't know who Mick Jagger is," I said. I wasn't nearly as much of a music lover as I was a politics lover.

"Do you think I can sit at the table next to his?" he asked.

"Sure," I said, and made the arrangement.

Mike sat next to Mick Jagger's table alone. I think he wanted to eavesdrop on some gossip.

Based on Mike's reaction to Mick Jagger being in the restaurant, I went to the table and introduced myself, but I didn't know which person at the table was the Rolling Stones singer. Feigning excitement, I asked the group as a whole if I could have a picture taken after their meal, and they said it wouldn't be a problem. Mick Jagger was in the picture. It turned out the band's drummer, Charlie Watts, was also at the restaurant with him. So was Keith Richards, the guitarist, who was kind of weird. He ran out of the restaurant before we took the picture. I learned later he was a different kind of guy from the rest of the band.

## SQUARE MOON

But one other person who didn't mind being photographed was Jerry Hall, the actress and model who was Mick Jagger's wife at the time.

While they were eating, Keith and Mick asked if it was alright if they smoked. Back then, smoking was still allowed in restaurants, but because they were in the basement dining room, where it was hard to circulate the air, I asked if they would mind smoking at the bar in back. Keith and Mick wound up taking turns every so often going from the table to the bar for cigarette breaks.

A lot of people said to me after that: "Wow, I can't believe you didn't let them smoke at the table. You should've let them do whatever they wanted." But I thought I should essentially treat them like everyone else. I think they kind of liked it that way because everywhere else they went people acted like they were gods or something.

I had a Polaroid picture taken and before it developed I asked Mick to sign it. He did and I took a Polaroid of him signing the Polaroid. Then, I started showing the photo of me with him to some of the regulars I knew who were sitting in the other dining room. They were so mad I didn't let them know the Rolling Stones were in the restaurant. "How could you not come and tell me?!" they said.

I responded, "Well, I didn't really know who he was."

If that wasn't exciting enough, the next day someone from *USA Today*, which at the time, I believe, was the only nationally circulated newspaper and the first to have color photos on the cover, came to City Lights of China. They were publishing a story about carry-out service, and while the reporter was there I pulled out the Rolling Stones Polaroid. The reporter, Nanci Hellmick, was so excited.

"Wow," she said. "When did that happen?"

I said, "Well, they were here last night," and I showed her where they sat.

"Can I borrow that picture?" she asked me.

"Sure," I said, "if you promise to give it back."

She agreed and, lo and behold, my photograph with Mick Jagger was on the front page of *USA Today* for everyone in the United States to see. I got phone calls from all over the country, people who traveled a lot for work who saw the paper and told me: "Next time Mick Jagger comes in you'd better tell me so that I can see him." All the TV networks called me and asked for an interview. One reporter, Mr. Art Campbell of the local NBC News 4, who did a regular segment about entertainment, came in, sat and talked with me. We also ordered everything that Mick Jagger ordered. He said he wanted to recreate my dinner with Mick. I was on TV. It was my three minutes of fame, I guess.

It all really showed me how big of a deal Mick Jagger was.

A week later, the Ritz Carlton called again and said Mick wanted to eat at City Lights of China before leaving for another city while on tour with the Rolling Stones.

"But," the caller said, "don't tell any press. If Mick sees the press outside, he won't come in."

I told them not to worry. I promised I wouldn't tell the press and, besides, I was a little burnt out on dealing with the media anyway. In came Mick Jagger with his children, who I immediately sat in a private area. I told him that he could smoke if he wanted to. Mick said that he would not smoke when his kids were around. I gave him my business card telling him that it was my great honor as a refugee from Vietnam to stand in front of the "King of Rock 'N' Roll." Mick said back: "No, Larry, don't say that, everyone's the same." Of course that's not true, but it's nice that he said so.

I walked around the restaurant and a few of my customers said to me, "Oh, Mick's back!"

"Yes, yes he is," I said, much, much more familiar with him than I had been a week earlier.

A few years later, I had the chance to serve another member of the Rolling Stones band, Ronnie Wood. Again, I did not know who he was until it was pointed out by another customer. Regardless, it meant that I'd met all the living Rolling Stones: Mick, Keith, Charlie and Ronnie.

\* \* \*

One morning I got to City Lights of China very early, before the restaurant opened. One of my workers opened the door for a woman who made her way all the way to the back of the restaurant where my office (and my historic phone) was located. She asked if I was Larry La, and when I said yes, she flashed a badge, said her name and then said "FBI" just like on TV.

"Oh, did I do something wrong?" I asked, taken aback.

She said I hadn't and she apologized for startling me. She explained she was there to case the place on behalf of the justice department. The Attorney General, Janet Reno, and Solicitor General, Drew Days, were planning on dining in at the restaurant that night. The agent wanted to know where the exits were and where they would sit. So I showed her and that night we had yet another Attorney General, our third, dined at City Lights of China — Reno and, previously, Bill Barr and Dick Thornburg. (A fourth Attorney General, Merrick B. Garland, would later become a customer of mine, too, at Meiwah restaurant.)

City Lights of China also welcomed a number of prominent business owners from all over the world. Among the most famous and successful was Herbert Haft, who was best known as a developer of discount stores, drug stores and bookstores, among other endeavors. He also owned a substantial head of hair that was all white.

One day, out of the blue, he called me to make a reservation. He wanted a table in 10 minutes, but we were so busy and I could not accommodate him in exactly that time frame. Fortunately, he understood and we pushed it back a little while. "In the future, if you can give us at least 30 minutes of advanced notice, I'll be able to take care of you more easily," I said.

By that point, City Lights of China had three different dining rooms. One of them was in the front of the restaurant, the only dining room where everyone who walked in could see the guests. Any time Mr. Haft booked a table at City Lights of China, he asked to sit in that particular space, even if that meant a little longer wait for him.

Whenever he'd exit the restaurant, he would tip me $5. I'm not sure that he realized I was an owner and instead maybe thought I was just a manager. As soon as he left I always gave the money to a staff member. One time, he saw me when he was leaving the restaurant, and he realized that he didn't have a $5 bill. He pulled out a $20 bill — and asked for change.

"Mr. Haft," I said. "Don't worry about it. You can give me double next time. Right now I don't have change on me."

"Make sure to remind me next time," he said.

The same thing happened another time, except he only had a $100 bill on him. He walked all the way to the cashier where I happened to be at the time to get change. I gave him the smaller bills, and he pulled out a $5 bill and handed it back to me.

"Mr. Haft, why don't you give me all of it?" I said jokingly.

"Oh, no," he said, pulling the small pile back quickly, almost like he feared I'd rip it from his hands.

But in spite of his thriftiness, Mr. Haft was a very staunch supporter of my restaurants until he passed away in 2004. He brought many people with him to eat my food through the years, which was helpful, not only in terms of immediate volume, but also from a marketing perspective. He always came with a very long limousine that was parked out front.

Sometimes he said he had to register a complaint with me.

"What was the problem?" I'd ask.

"Your food portion is too big, and your price is too low," he'd say kiddingly.

He was helping to spread the word about the businesses, so sometimes I'd undercharge Mr. Haft for services without minding so much.

One such instance was when he asked me to cater a reception at his home, where he was hosting 80 guests. He just wanted me to provide finger foods, like egg rolls, for the cocktail hour. He asked me the price and off the top of my head I said, "$10 per person," which I thought was quite reasonable.

"Now, Larry," Mr. Haft said. "I hope you're not taking advantage of our friendship."

At first, I thought that might've meant he thought I was going easy on him, but I quickly realized he suspected I was actually trying to gouge him.

"How about $1 less? Nine dollars per person," I said. That made him very happy.

He asked me, "So, it is going to be $720 total?"

"Yes, sir," I said.

"Give me your hand," he said.

I went to shake it, and he said, "How about $700 even?"

I said, "Deal, Mr. Haft."

He was very happy that he could haggle me down another $20. I think to him, it was not the amount of money that mattered, but the idea that he always made good deals.

Mr. Haft wasn't the only City Lights of China regular who liked sitting in the front dining room. Mr. Jack Kent Cooke, the owner of the NFL team then known as the Washington Redskins, always asked to sit in that area, too. In fact, he only sat at one of the tables next to the front window, even though we were in a basement space and not too many people were looking down into the restaurant from the street. When you looked out of the window, you didn't see much more than the legs of passersby either. But that was Mr. Cooke's preference, and he always gave advanced notice so we could save a window seat for him.

I knew him when he was in his 80s, and he was still very energetic, always speaking loudly. He brought his fourth wife with him as well as her son.

Like Mr. Haft, Mr. Cooke was a billionaire who was also very careful with his money. He negotiated with the D.C. government so hard over the cost of a new stadium that he had to settle for one in the state of Maryland instead. It took quite a long time for the new stadium to be built bearing his name, Jack Kent Cooke Stadium. By the time it opened, unfortunately he'd passed away.

We had a unique payment arrangement with him, too, where we sent invoices to his office in Middleburg, a town in Virginia, once a month. When Mr. Kent Cooke died, there was an outstanding bill, but we sent an invoice to his office and it got paid right away. I think that says something about the level of organization that existed in his successful company.

*Sponsored by First Baptist church in Erwin, Tennessee*

*First House in USA - Erwin, TN*

# LARRY TRUNG LA

*Erwin Record, the local newspaper in Erwin*

*East Tennessee State University*

*Honored graduate with Mom*

*ETSU President, VP and First Lady*

*Trung Van La with Fred 'Honkey' Davis and Barbara*

*City Lights of China in the 1990s*

*Dad's last birthday celebration with 8 siblings at City Lights*

*Mom's 80th birthday at Meiwah*

*Getting married in Miami, 1988*

*UNHCR High Commissioners OGATA, ROOYEN*

*Rolling Stones on USA Today at City Lights*

*My family with Mom*

*Nancy Pelosi, House Speaker*

*Meiwah D.C. opened in 2000*

*Senators Ted Kennedy and Harry Reid*

# CHAPTER 6

After getting settled at City Lights of China, my wife Diana and I settled into a home located in a northern suburb of Washington D.C., Montgomery County, part of the great state of Maryland. We've lived in the area, now, for more than 35 years.

In 1990, Diana and I welcomed our first child, Alisa, into the world. She was always a curious girl, so once Alisa was old enough to go places, even events where D.C. power players were on the guest list, I'd bring her along. My wife enjoys such occasions far less, because I always go around the room and talk to everybody, so it was nice to have some company with Alisa by my side.

I think this helped Alisa become comfortable talking to different kinds of people, especially individuals who are much older than she. At home, Alisa always sat on my lap and watched the news, so I guess, considering all this, it's not shocking that she ended up working in politics. Her first Federal Government job was as an intern at the age of 16 at the Labor Department while she was in high school. During the summer of her junior year, she became a page at the Senate, and then in college she scored an internship at the Office of the Chief of Protocol, Department of State. She did so well there she got a job in that Office after college, which required a security clearance that took months to obtain, even though she was only 21 years old at the time. When she finally went in for her first day of work, her boss jokingly asked, "Did you kill somebody, why did it take so long for your security clearance?"

Alisa was in the Office of the Chief of Protocol through Hillary Clinton's time as Secretary of State and then Secretary John Kerry. Alisa always dreamed of working on a Presidential campaign. When Mrs. Clinton ran for President in 2015, Alisa leapt at the chance to work on that campaign. So she moved to Brooklyn, New York, where the campaign was headquartered, for a year and a half. I encouraged her to do that since it might be a once in a lifetime opportunity.

After the election, in 2017, Alisa eventually got a job working for Leader Pelosi, who a year later became Speaker of the House. Alisa worked as Speaker Pelosi's personal assistant for five years. Afterward, Alisa moved on to a position with a private company.

Diana gave birth to Timothy in 1993, and though we love him all the same, of course, he's the exact opposite of Alisa. He's very smart, but not quite as outgoing, which probably explains why he ended up working in IT. Diana and I are extremely proud of the man he has become, even if it means in life he voluntarily flies well under the radar, so to speak.

* * *

I ran City Lights of China from 1988 until 1998. I worked at least six days a week, every week there, and I was proud to have improved the state of the business so much during that time.

Though the restaurant business is one that I enjoy a lot, it's not an easy business to be in.

One rainy night, we had many delivery orders stuck inside the restaurant because the drivers couldn't get around as quickly as usual. I grabbed a bag that was already very late and left to deliver it myself. Since I did not know the road where the home was located very well, and it was dark and raining so heavily, I had to get out of the car to look for the right door. I got soaked to the skin while wearing a shirt and tie. When I showed up to the customer's home, he opened the door with a very angry face, which I expected. I gave him the bag and apologized for being so late. I told him the food was free tonight. He did not say a word, grabbed the bag of food and slammed the door in my face.

I stood there for a few seconds wondering how he could do that to someone who got so wet trying to bring him food. I called him back the following night to apologize again, even though I was treated badly. This time, he felt very uneasy talking to me since he did not expect me to call him back to apologize once again for what happened the night before. But, he was our customer after all, and in the restaurant business you have to have good "people skills."

The majority of the customers are very good, but some are classified as "high maintenance" — the kind where, pretty much no matter what you do for them, they are not happy. I told my staff not to look at such customers as a problem, but as a challenge. If you can make them happy, everyone else becomes easier to serve. (I also told them to always keep the dining room as clean as possible because when customers come in and see a dirty dining room, they also imagine a filthy kitchen.)

Still, most customers are not meddlesome at all, but after 10 years in a basement commercial space, I started to feel a little suffocated. So much about the restaurant was incredible, but I needed a little bit of a change, if only in location. Basement life is not fun. The ceiling was so low, I could jump up and touch it. Sometimes in the afternoon when I'd walk into the street to run an errand after being in the restaurant for so long, I had this strange feeling that I could easily jump up and touch the sky. My depth perception was affected that much.

I asked my partners if they wanted to move the restaurant to another location on street level, build a new location somewhere else, or sell it. They decided not to move the City Lights of China, or build a new restaurant, because both of those maneuvers were too risky and expensive. So, I sold my shares of the restaurant to new owners, and I went on vacation — to Vietnam.

I wanted to see the country of my birth for the first time in 20 years. When I got there, it was very different from how I remembered it. Relations between the U.S. and Vietnam were normalized in 1995, which immensely helped the economy there. The area where I lived most of my boyhood had dramatically improved from the last time I'd seen it. There were new investors showing up and they were building new buildings. The country started to feel like it was becoming modernized.

I saw the house where I grew up. The market was still in front of it, but my old home was under government control and used as an office headquarters. I had the opportunity to go inside, actually, because my old neighbor was still living next door and he knew the government officials working there. I still recognized all the rooms in which I ran around with my siblings.

I also saw friends and relatives who were still living there. They told me that in the years after I'd left, the country struggled economically so much. Even if you had money in the early 1980s in Vietnam, there wasn't a whole lot to buy in stores, they said. But many of them were doing better financially — though others experienced hardship.

It was an emotional trip for me. Overall, I had an amazing time before returning to my chosen home.

# SQUARE MOON

*  *  *

As much as I appreciated spending more time with my family, it wasn't long before I got a little stir crazy — and, frankly, even a bit bored. By the end of 1998 after my first trip back to Vietnam after 20 years, I missed working, even though running a restaurant was very difficult at times. I was only 42 years old, too early to retire, and the thing I longed for the most was interactions with my customers and my staff.

A little while after I returned from Vietnam, I spoke to some of my former staff members at City Lights of China. They were not too happy with the new owner of the restaurant and said they wanted to work for me in a new Chinese restaurant in Washington D.C.

"No, you won't work *for* me," I insisted. "You'll work *with* me, as partners in our new restaurant."

One of the primary chefs from City Lights of China along with the kitchen manager pooled together their savings. Combined with the money I had we were close to having enough to open a restaurant together, but we still needed a little bit more. We decided to seek a loan from a bank to help with construction costs. Banks do not like to grant construction loans to restaurants. Approximately 60 percent of restaurants fail within the first year of operation and 80 percent fail within the first three years. In part because of this, banks always require collateral for such large loans. For my new venture, I put up my house as collateral. If the restaurant failed, I'd be homeless, but I had confidence we'd succeed.

It took us a while to find a space and negotiate a lease. Once we moved in, it took us more than a year to build the restaurant because the property was totally bare. But we eventually opened Meiwah restaurant at 1200 New Hampshire Avenue in February 2000.

I was so anxious to open the new place. We were so successful with City Lights of China and I wanted to at least equal that success. But you never know how a new restaurant will be received. Plus, I had to compete with the famous City Lights of China!

It was fortunate that we were busy on Day One when we put the "Grand Opening" sign up. Word had already spread around town that Larry La from City Lights of China was opening a new restaurant in the West End area. We called it Meiwah.

On one of the many special occasions my staff and I were asked to provide food, I got the chance to explain the meaning of the name. The event was held at the Blair House, the official guest house of the President of the United States. The theme of the evening's menu was "Taste of China" and one of the primary guests was the Chinese Ambassador to the U.S., Zhang Yesui. He asked me what the name meant and I told him, "Mei means 'America' and wah means 'China,' and both countries are so important to each other and to the world that we can't afford to have any kind of war, either a military conflict or an economic conflict. So the name is Meiwah to inspire a coming together of the two countries, over food, in any time of conflict to keep the peace."

The Ambassador was so pleased with that answer. He said, "You're right, we need to have peace, no matter what."

(There are times when tensions between the U.S. and China are so profound that I admit it would probably take more than a meal to smooth them over. We'd probably have to at least throw in a case of Tsing Tao beer, too.)

I liked the location of Meiwah a lot more than I did the space in which City Lights of China existed. There, we were in the basement, but at Meiwah we were at street level, in a corner lot, with dining rooms on two floors, seating 150 people. At City Lights we relied on a single window to attract customers, but the Meiwah space had ten 18-foot floor-to-ceiling glass windows wrapping around the building. Everyone who walked by — on portions of two blocks — could look in and see the food and the atmosphere. In her review, Ms. Phyllis Richman of the *Washington Post*, noted the big, red neon sign in front and called the place "homey" but also "modern and sleek," which I liked. People passed through nine-foot-high Chinese-style ancient gates, which really set the tone, and we built a menu that was nearly identical to the one at City Lights of China. My partners and I thought: why change something that worked so well?

Washington D.C. is a pretty small town in a way. Just like I could always recall the names of people in the refugee camp when I helped Madame Ann with her paperwork for the Malaysian Red Crescent, I remembered the names of many of my customers from City Lights of China. They always appreciated it. I asked my old City Lights customers to dine with us, day one, at Meiwah, and they arrived with smiles.

We had a grand opening party one week after we opened for business. We closed the restaurant that weekend and only allowed a few hundred invited guests to join us.

One person who was there at Meiwah that opening weekend was Vice President Al Gore's Chief of Staff, Mr. Charles Burson, a Tennessee native. He was actually eating at the carry-out corner. I apologized and told him I'd get him a table, and he said, "No! Don't worry about me. Take care of your other customers." He was so kind and humble.

Later that year, after the Presidential Election was awarded to George W. Bush over Al Gore by the U.S. Supreme Court, and Mr. Gore's support staff were exiting the White House, Mr. Burson called and asked if I could send some food over.

"A lot of people are helping us move out, we need to feed them," he said. "They want food from Meiwah."

He also told me that he pasted the Meiwah takeout menu on the Vice President Chief of Staff's office wall. "If anyone wants to take it down, they're going to have to take down the whole wall," he said.

It was a funny thing for him to say, but it showed how much support my restaurants had through the years, and for that I'm so grateful.

Senate Majority Leader Harry Reid was another regular at Meiwah, in part because he lived across the street from the restaurant at the Ritz Carlton Residence, a high-end condominium. He came into the restaurant one time with a few guests and his staff, and we sat him upstairs in a private room. He remarked that the space was very nice and that he'd like to hold meetings there sometime. When he told me that, I remembered that it was Mr. Reid who convinced Senator Jim Jeffords, Vermont, to change his political party affiliation, from Republican to Independent, on the Senate floor. That move shifted Senate majority power away from the Republicans.

"Senator Reid," I said, "the next time you want to convince a Senator to change parties, you can do that here in the restaurant." I got him to chuckle at that one.

Eventually he and I became close enough to where I felt comfortable telling him that I always wanted to meet Senator Ted Kennedy. Mr. Reid asked me why and I told him that when I came to this great country, I'd read an article saying it was Senator Kennedy who heavily supported legislation that doubled the quota of refugees admitted to the United States from Indochina. That paved the way for me and my family to come into the United States earlier than we could have otherwise. I always wanted to thank Senator Kennedy in person for pushing that bill across the line.

## SQUARE MOON

Mr. Reid immediately turned to one of his staff members and said, "Arrange that."

Two weeks later I got a call from Mr. Reid's office saying that they coordinated a time for my family and I to go to the Capitol Building and meet Senator Kennedy. I was so excited, not only for myself, but my family, who joined me, including one of my brothers, Jim, who came to the U.S. from Vietnam alongside me and has worked for NASA for more than 30 years.

We had to wait a while to meet him, though. The Senate was in the middle of a filibuster that day. (Washington wasn't going to completely stop just for me!) My family and I were in Senator Reid's office, and I think some of his staff recognized we were getting restless after such a long time. To keep us entertained, they escorted us to the Senate Gallery where we could see the action. Senator Kennedy himself was filibustering away, reading from his notes. He was arguing against the appointment of Miguel Estrada as a federal judge because he believed Estrada did not have enough experience to exhibit a consistent legal philosophy. It was amazing to see the Senate in action.

When the filibuster was finally over, my family and I were shuffled back to Mr. Reid's office. Soon, in walked Senator Ted Kennedy from Massachusetts, the man who made my whole life in America possible. We were so jazzed when he appeared. He'd been in the Senate for a long time and introduced so many critical pieces of legislation that helped shape history — and helped shape the lives of individual people. How many of them ever got the chance to directly tell him about the impact his work has had on their lives? In the grand scheme of things, I imagine it hasn't been too many.

As excited as I was to meet him, he seemed equally as excited. (In fact, I *know* he was, because a few months later, we catered an event for

Senator Dick Durbin from Illinois. I introduced myself to him as "Larry La from Meiwah restaurant," and Senator Durbin immediately said, "Are you the refugee from Vietnam that Ted talked about?") I expressed my appreciation to Senator Kennedy for what he did for refugees. He said he was grateful to hear that and then asked what I was doing with myself. I told him I'd managed City Lights of China and that I now owned Meiwah. I pointed to Mr. Reid and said, "He's one of my very best customers, actually."

Then, Senator Kennedy became yet another cherished regular at Meiwah. My daughter, Alisa, was a page in the Senate while in high school. In the "L" shaped cloakroom, Senator Kennedy told a few other Senators, who were facing a long night of work, that they should order dinner from Meiwah. Alisa was obscured on the other side of the "L" shaped room, the cloakroom staff at the corner saw her but she was too shy to avail herself. The staffer motioned over to Alisa to come over and said, "Senator Kennedy, the owner's daughter is actually right here. She works as a page."

"Can you call your dad and put in an order for us?" Senator Kennedy asked. Of course, she couldn't refuse!

"Hey Dad," Alisa said to me over the phone a minute later. "Senator Kennedy wants to order some food for the Senators who are working late."

"Sure, I'll take care of that," I said — not that there was anything else I could say as a good D.C. business owner.

Senator Kennedy remained a customer of ours until he got sick and unfortunately passed away. He was so kind to us. My respect for him only grew over the years.

At our U.S. Capitol, when the House of Representatives worked late, the Majority Whip or Minority Whip often ordered food from

Meiwah for House members and their staffers to eat in the Whip office. The meal for around 200 to 250 people was always paid for by the Whip office. Early in the day we were asked to "standby" since they were not sure whether they all would have to stay late. By around 3 p.m. the call came in to give us the green light to start cooking. We'd deliver the food in two hours to the U.S. Capitol Building.

We had a different protocol with Senators, in part because individual Senators pay for dinner if he or she wants their colleagues to stay late and discuss their bill.

So, we took care of both Chambers, and both parties. In business, we do not take sides politically, everyone is our customer.

* * *

Supreme Court Justice Elena Kagan became a regular at Meiwah, but I vividly remember the first time she visited. She came with Judge David Tatel and Judge Patricia Wald, both of whom served on the D.C. Circuit. Judge Tatel introduced me to Justice Kagan and Judge Wald, and I made sure to seat them in a comfortable booth. They enjoyed a wonderful lunch together.

During her Senate confirmation hearings in 2010, after President Obama nominated her to the seat, Senator Lindsay Graham from South Carolina asked her where she'd spent the prior Christmas. He was referring to the day Al-Qaeda tried — and failed — to set off a bomb on board a plane traveling to Detroit. (That was the so-called "Underpants Bomber" incident.) The eventual Justice Kagan said, "Like all Jews, I was probably at a Chinese restaurant." Everyone in the chamber laughed and it might've been the single biggest highlight of the hearings.

Weeks later, I met Senator Graham at an event. I told him, "When you asked Justice Kagan where she was on Christmas Day, and she said, 'at a Chinese restaurant,' you should've asked a follow-up question."

"Oh yeah," the Senator said. "What would that have been?"

"*Which* Chinese restaurant?" I said. "Then she would've said, 'Meiwah restaurant.' I should've written you all a script!"

He laughed and said, "Senators don't follow a script. We say what we want to say." (That is very true.)

As for judges in town, I have two favorites who frequently visited Meiwah for years.

One of them is Judge David Tatel, Senior Judge of the United States Court of Appeals for the District of Columbia Circuit. Judge Tatel became blind before the age of 30 due to retinitis pigmentosa. He was appointed by President Clinton to the Court of Appeals in 1994, and on his 10th anniversary in the role, he got 40 clerks together for dinner at Meiwah. I was invited to Judge Tatel's chamber where, together, we had a picture taken. He told me that I could attend the court proceeding that day. I really wanted to see how Judge Tatel conducted his court as a blind person. He seemed extremely focused on the cases presented before him. As one of three judges, he asked more questions than anyone. I really admire him beyond words.

I got to know the Judge and his whole family, including his uncle, Ambassador Morton Abramowitz, and his late mother, Molly. They were all regulars. I always had a birthday cake for Molly with the words "Happy Birthday, Judge's Mom." She really liked to be addressed that way. (Who *isn't* proud to have a distinguished son like that?) When Judge Tatel published his memoir, VISION, A Memoir of Blindness and Justice, I was so honored to attend the celebration of its release. U.S. Supreme Court Justice Sonia Sotomayor came to this special event along with many other judges, active and retired, as well as a number of prominent lawyers in town. Nina Totenberg, the famous legal affairs correspondent for National Public Radio, was there, too. There were many people at the event so I did not wait for my book to be autographed. I told the Judge that, instead, he could sign my book at the Meiwah sushi bar when he and his wife, Edie, visited next. I finally got his book autographed at our restaurant.

Another of my favorite judges is Judge Florence Yu Pan, the United States Circuit Judge of the United States Court of Appeals for the District of Columbia. I got to know Judge Pan over the course of more than 20 years. Meiwah has had the great honor of catering many special occasions for her and her family, such as her wedding reception in 2004 at the Embassy of New Zealand. Meiwah also supplied food for her first investiture as a judge, when she became Judge of the Superior Court of the District of Columbia in 2009, and her investiture as United States Circuit Judge in 2022. We also catered the Bar Mitzvah of one of her sons and other events at her home. I got to know her husband, Max, and their two sons very well. One is attending Yale University and the other is on their way to Stanford University, where his parents attended law school. It's an honor for Meiwah — and me — to call members of this wonderful family friends for so many years.

Another regular of both City Lights of China and Meiwah restaurants in the Academic world is Stephen Trachtenberg, the former President of George Washington University for 19 years. I got to know Mr. Trachtenberg and his family well for many decades. When he retired from GWU presidency in 2007, he was succeeded by Dr. Steven Knapp. Dr. Knapp and his wife, Diana, are also a Meiwah regular customer. At his inauguration as the 16th President of GWU, I attended the event as a "stand-in" for my alma mater's President, Dr.

Paul Stanton, Jr. What an honor to march to this special occasion together with presidents of many Universities and Colleges. The year that Dr. Steven Knapp became the GWU President in 2008, my daughter, Alisa, also was admitted to this University.

# CHAPTER 7

When I think about all the people I have been able to meet, simply because I was able to manage some restaurants in Washington D.C., the capital of this great nation, it is hard for me to believe. Considering where I came from and what my family and I had to endure, it's difficult not to feel a tremendous sense of pride, while retaining a lot of humility. When I actually began to meet *Presidents*, that was when my success really became clear.

Every summer while Bill Clinton was in office at the White House, the Clintons threw what they called a Congressional Picnic, inviting members of both the House of Representatives and the Senate. There were Democrats *and* Republicans there, and it was a time when both sides talked to each other in a civil way, even if they did not agree with each other on the floor of the Senate or the House.

The picnic was an all-you-can-eat-and-drink-party in the White House's South Lawn. As a local businessman, then in charge of Meiwah restaurant. I was invited to attend. President Clinton's Deputy Assistant, Doug Band, was one of the best customers we had at Meiwah restaurant. He was the one who called in the orders for the White House and was the man kind enough to get me an invite to the Congressional Picnic in the last year of the Clinton White House.

One of President Clinton's aides, Bruce Lindsey, was another frequent customer at City Lights of China. He told me many people who work in the White House ate the restaurant's food, but when they made delivery orders they didn't provide their real names. I guessed that meant the people were pretty high up!

The person at the picnic who most impressed my daughter Alisa, age 9 at that time, was no politician. It was the actor Chevy Chase, who she'd seen in a number of movies growing up. She excitedly ran up to him and he kindly talked to her. My friend Ralph Alswang took three photos of the two of them together, my daughter shaking hands with him, and Mr. Chase giving her a hug as she smiles ear to ear.

While in attendance at the picnic, I also saw Max Cleland, the Georgia Senator who was a disabled U.S. Army veteran. Unfortunately, he lost most of each of his legs and half of his right arm when a grenade exploded in front of him during the Vietnam War. I knew all about his background, and I approached him at the party.

"Senator, my name is Larry La," I said to him. "Thank you so much for all you did for my country during the war. We have so much appreciation for the servicemen who helped." I always felt bad about the war because so many young people had to go far away from home in America to fight a war that was unwinnable. It was in a country where there were many guerilla soldiers and no one knew who the enemy was and who their friends were.

He was very touched by that, and a few days later I got a handwritten note from him. He thanked me for my remarks and asked if my family and I would like to visit his office in the Senate. Of course I wanted to!

My wife joined me, and so did my kids. It was important for me to have them meet a man like him and see the kinds of sacrifices people have to make in war. I also wanted them to see how certain people can also overcome adversity. Here was a pretty severely disabled man actually serving in the U.S. Senate. That was incredible and he set a great example. From that moment on, I became very close to Senator Cleland. Meiwah hosted a fundraiser for his reelection, though, unfortunately, he did not win a second term. However, after his time in the Senate, he was appointed by President Obama to the board of directors of the Export-Import Bank of the United States. Anytime he came to D.C. from Georgia, he stopped by Meiwah to see me.

At the Congressional Picnic, I also met the President, Bill Clinton, himself. He came outside to the party and we shook hands. We spoke briefly and told him that I'd sent and served many, many meals to members of his cabinet.

After he left the White House, Mr. Clinton and his wife Hillary — who was elected as a New York Senator in 2000, just as Bill was leaving his office — remained customers of mine. Around then, Huma Abedin, who was Hillary's aide and later Deputy Chief of Staff when Hillary was Secretary of State, often called-in their orders to the restaurant on their behalf. Anytime the Clintons ordered from Meiwah while they were down in Washington from New York — with their daughter Chelsea, too — I always accompanied the delivery driver. I knew there would be Secret Service at their residence and I didn't want anyone to worry about who was ringing the doorbell. I always told the driver to drive slowly and straight so as not to raise attention or suspicion.

One time in 2001, I rang the bell at the Clinton house and briefly turned my back to the door. Suddenly behind me, the door opened up, and a very recognizable voice said, "How much do I owe you?" I turned around and it was President Clinton himself. "Oh, Mr. President!" I said. It was the first time I saw him up close wearing casual clothes: jeans and a t-shirt. It was very disorienting.

I waved the driver over to present the food. Mr. Clinton pulled out his wallet from his jeans, and I watched his face concentrate on the receipt as he figured out an appropriate tip for the driver. It took a little while. I bet it wasn't terribly often he needed to worry about such trivialities while in the White House. (He tipped about 25 percent, which was pretty good, by the way.)

When I went back to Meiwah, I told some customers what happened. Then, the next day, I got a call from the *Washington Post* to verify the story. I guess one of my customers told on me. Not only did that story run in the *Post*, but the *International Herald Tribune*, too, which the *Post* owned and delivered news to the entire world. Meiwah customers were calling me from all over the world to tell me they saw the article. That was pretty incredible and I think showed that he was a pretty popular President.

I'm convinced that Bill Clinton liked my restaurant's food so much that he recommended it to other people — the kinds of individuals who are ordinarily in his orbit, that is. In 2002, President George W. Bush asked Mr. Clinton to represent the U.S. at the inauguration of the newly designated country East Timor. The Prime Minister for East Timor was Mari Alkatiri, and when he made his first trip to Washington D.C. a few months later, he came to Meiwah, of all places, for dinner. Mr. Alkatiri came back for lunch the next day, just after meeting with Secretary of State Colin Powell. I'd seen them on TV together earlier, and Mr. Alkatiri was wearing the same suit and tie, so I recognized him immediately. He must've liked both of those meals quite a bit, because he then came back a third time for an additional meal on the same trip.

Unwittingly, Bill Clinton also helped me get out of driving tickets.

One time President Clinton ordered Meiwah when he was in town to deliver a eulogy at Arlington National Cemetery for General John

Shalikashvili, who was the Chairman of the Joint Chiefs of Staff while Mr. Clinton was in office. First, I drove the order over to the cemetery, with a member of the Secret Service in the passenger seat.

"Are you sure we can drive around Arlington Cemetery?" I asked him.

He flashed his badge back at me and said, "Yes, we can."

But we got there too late. Mr. Clinton's motorcade had left.

I then got a call from President Clinton's aide telling me to deliver the food to the Dulles International Airport where Mr. Clinton's chartered flight would be waiting. It was a Friday afternoon and I knew traffic was going to be bad. But I had to deliver, literally. (And deliver a lot of food, too, because whenever Mr. Clinton ordered from my restaurant for a chartered flight, he fed everyone on board.)

I was about five minutes away from the airport when the traffic loosened up and I sped up my car — too much, apparently. I heard a siren behind me, saw a police car in my rearview mirror and thought, "Oh no."

I pulled over, took out my driver's license and waited for the officer. When he got to my window I said, "Sir, I'm so sorry that I might have driven too fast. You don't have to believe what I am going to tell you, but I will tell you anyway. I am delivering food to our former President."

He didn't say a word. He just took my license and walked back to his vehicle to check my record. A few minutes later, he came back and asked, "Do you know how fast you were driving?"

"No sir," I said.

He told me, "83 miles per hour."

I knew that in Virginia if you drove a certain amount over the speed limit, it wouldn't just be a speeding ticket, it would mean a charge of reckless driving, which was much worse. I thought for a moment I was in real trouble and maybe was destined for jail.

Good thing I had a clean driving record. He let me off with a warning, and said, "You drive more carefully now."

I thanked him. I imagine that he believed my story because law enforcement in the area probably knows when dignitaries like former Presidents are in town. I called the aide to apologize for running so late. I told him that I wouldn't have time to deliver the food after going through the terminal, so he drove out to meet me in front. I passed bags of food from my car's window through his.

Another time I got a call to deliver food to President Clinton at the Hilton Hotel in Washington D.C. By then a former President — though those who've held that office are forever referred to as "President" — President Clinton made a speech to commemorate 9/11. After that he had to fly back to New York City for another 9/11-focused event. He finished his remarks a little bit early, and I did not realize that his motorcade was waiting for our food in the hotel's parking garage. That Hotel Hilton was the place President Ronald Reagan was leaving when John Hinckley, Jr. wounded him in an assassination attempt. Since then, anytime a President was in the hotel, the garage was locked down. No one could come in or leave until the motorcade left.

Eventually I made my way over there at the scheduled time and delivered the food. After I got back to the restaurant, I got a call from a *New York Post* reporter who also was a frequent guest at Meiwah. He asked if I'd just brought food to President Clinton.

"Yes," I said. "How did you know that?"

"You delayed everyone from leaving the garage since the President's motorcade was still inside waiting for your food."

I was on the "Page 6" of the *New York Post* the next day.

# SQUARE MOON

\* \* \*

The day President Clinton was in town to mark was one of the most challenging days in the history of Meiwah: September 11, 2001. There was the destruction in New York, but the Pentagon in Washington D.C. was also attacked, and nobody was sure what would happen next. As White House Chief of Staff Andrew Card told President Bush that day in Florida, America was under attack, so many people in the city fled out of fear.

I was back at home in Silver Spring, Maryland, and, after picking my kids up from school, I drove right to Meiwah. It certainly was a frightening day, but I think my childhood in Vietnam prepared me for it. My focus was to be there for my staff — and my customers. I drove to D.C. while everyone else was getting out of the city. There was only my car and government vehicles on the road in my lane.

When I got to the restaurant, our Manager, Bob, from Taiwan, who'd never experienced any war in his life, was scared. He was about to instruct everyone to go home, which I understood to some extent, but my instincts were different. I locked the doors and told the staff to stay calm inside the restaurant. At the time, we didn't really know the whole story about what was happening to the country. Besides, the traffic was so bad leaving the city, they might as well sit in the cozy restaurant instead of the cramped front seats of their cars.

If any of my employees didn't want to come to work or couldn't make it, that was completely fine, of course. In fact, one of my staff members called and said she was going to be late because the traffic was so bad. "Find an exit, turn around and go home," I said, curtly just because I wanted to stress that work did not have to be a number one priority. She misunderstood my intention and for a second thought I was firing her. "No, no, I'll be there as soon as I can!" she said. But I told her to just go home and watch the news and that we might not open for business at all.

My staff — of which 90 percent showed up to work — and I hung out with the restaurant's doors locked for a while. We watched the news and waited to see what happened next. After some time, customers started showing up and many others called for delivery orders. We were one of very few restaurants that were open, maybe even the *only* one that was open in the area that day.

With the airports shut down and so many people stuck in D.C., it was a very busy day at Meiwah. People didn't want to sit in their hotel rooms, alone and depressed. Unsurprisingly, we sold more adult beverages that day than any other in the history of the restaurant. Almost everyone had a drink in their hand. So many customers came up to me and said, "I'm so appreciative that you opened up for us today." It was amazing to see people standing around the bar, talking to strangers, and sitting at dinner tables, comforting one another.

\* \* \*

At Meiwah in D.C. there was a "Wall of Fame": a collection of pictures of me with esteemed restaurant guests, of which there were many. There was Senator Tammy Duckworth, born in Bangkok, Thailand, who represents the state of Illinois; Susan Rice, the National Security Advisor for President Obama; Senator Edward Markey from Massachusetts; and Nancy Pelosi, two-time Speaker of the House, and one-time boss of my daughter.

Speaker Pelosi once threw a party at her office to celebrate the marriage of one of her staffers and my daughter Alisa's engagement. I was invited and the shindig took place a few months after Speaker Pelosi had to stand in front of the chamber for eight consecutive hours during a filibuster, with nothing to eat and probably only water to drink. I approached her and said, "Sorry Leader Pelosi, I watched only five hours of your speech that day." She laughed, lifted one of her legs and pointed to her shoe. "And I had to stand in high heels the whole time, too!" she said.

On the Meiwah Wall of Fame was also CNN news anchor Dana Bash who signed her photo: "I can't live without Meiwah dumplings." I have known Dana for many decades since she has been our regular and loves our vegetarian dumplings. When I drove to Philadelphia for the DNC Convention in 2016 where Dana covered the event for CNN, I brought a whole tray of vegetarian dumplings and dropped off at her hotel for her.

Joie Chen, an Asian American broadcast journalist, is a good friend that I got to know for a long time. I was a big fan of her on TV news. I watched her on CNN when she was the anchor for CNN in Atlanta before I met her in person when she became a Washington-based correspondent for CBS News. She has been Meiwah's loyal customer for many years. Joie won many Emmy Awards. She was our keynote speaker when we launched the Asian American Chamber of Commerce that I co-founded. Last October, Joie was kind enough to introduce me at the Chinese American Museum to receive the 2023 Gold Lantern Awards held at the Kennedy Center. What an honor to know such an extraordinary Asian American whom I am really proud to consider as a great friend.

James Wolfensohn, who was President of the World Bank and Chairman of the Kennedy Center, was also photographed for the wall. I once kidded Mr. Wolfensohn, who sold his investment banking company for $210 million in the 1990s after becoming the President of the World Bank, that he seemed to be doing pretty well financially. "Yes, it means I can eat at your restaurant more often," he said. I responded: "Oh, Mr. Wolfensohn, you could buy this restaurant many times over if you chose to do so," which provoked a laugh out of both of us.

He became a regular customer, introducing me to dinner guests of his like Paul Volcker, who was Chairman of the Federal Reserve Bank, and Alan Greenspan, who succeeded Mr. Volcker in that position. Chairman Greenspan and his wife, Andrea Mitchell, were guests of Mr. Wolfensohn. When I approached their table, Mr. Wolfensohn introduced me to Andrea Mitchell, who turned to her husband sitting next to her and said, "This is my famous husband, the Chairman." To that I replied, "Do you know that the Chairman was more famous after April 1994?" Andrea had no clue what I meant. She thought it might be the day that one of the Chairman's comments caused the stock market to crash. But that was another year. After a pause, the Chairman told his wife, "He remembers and you don't?" I was actually referring to the day they got married. We all laughed.

When Mr. Wolfensohn and Mr. Greenspan received their bill for the dinner, a friendly debate over who would pay erupted. Mr. Wolfensohn insisted first, but Mr. Greenspan won the argument.

"No, put it on my credit card," Mr. Greenspan said. "I'll just lower the interest rates" — quite a funny joke considering he had the power to actually do that.

\* \* \*

In addition to the Rolling Stones, another musician I got to know through my ownership of restaurants was Lang Lang, a Chinese pianist who has performed with major orchestras around the world and appeared onstage at many well-known concert halls dating back to when he was 17 years old. In 2003, I was asked to cook Chinese food at the residence of D.C. lawyer Stephen Porter for a private concert featuring Lang Lang. There were 30 guests at the Porter home, all of whom were prominent D.C. figures, including Supreme Court Justice Scalia; President Bill Clinton's lawyer, Bob Bennett; and François Bujon de l'Estang, the French Ambassador to the U.S. I was so impressed with the young Lang Lang for being able to perform in front of so many dignitaries, and in such an intimate setting. On this special occasion, I also brought Alisa with me since she turned 13 that day. Mrs. Susan Porter, Stephen's wife, knew about the occasion and told Lang Lang. What a wonderful surprise it was to have Lang Lang play "Happy Birthday" for Alisa at the end of his set. Everyone sang along.

Mr. Bob Bennett, our Meiwah regular, told me, "Larry, how many 13-year-old kids have a U.S. Supreme Court Justice sing 'Happy Birthday' to them?"

"That is very true, what an honor for Alisa!" I replied.

The following year at another event also at the Porter's residence, his car service did not show up to take him to George Mason University as planned, Alisa and I volunteered to take Lang Lang and his father in my "half-size limousine." Alisa was so nervous to sit in the backseat with the famous Lang Lang, especially since she just saw him being interviewed on the Jay Leno show the night before. Lang Lang had been grateful to me at that moment.

Lang Lang became yet another Meiwah loyal customer. He would never come to D.C. without visiting Meiwah. Once, after a performance at the Kennedy Center, Lang Lang came to Meiwah with the conductor of the National Symphony Orchestra. Customers, who'd just seen him on stage, asked him for autographs and pictures. Lang Lang was such a nice gentleman in accommodating them, especially some children.

Another time, there was a special program in town for which Lang Lang stayed for eight days, which was a long time for him. Usually he was in and out of town after a day or two, tops. In that eight-day stretch he ate nine different meals at Meiwah. His favorite dish was our Beijing Duck.

Every time Lang Lang was in D.C. to perform, at events like the National Memorial Day Concert or the Independence Day concert produced by PBS called "A Capitol Fourth," I always got tickets from Lang Lang. I told Lang Lang a few times that I enjoy the fact that he lets his personality shine onstage. He has a flamboyant, theatrical style of playing that I can appreciate even more than what he's doing on a technical level at the piano. I am so proud to know Lang Lang and to call him as a friend for more than 20 years.

*　*　*

The Supreme Court's Chief Justice John Roberts was also on Meiwah's Wall of Fame, and is central to an interesting story. Every month I went to get a haircut at a strip mall in the Washington D.C. suburb Falls Church, Virginia. It was called the Eden Center and it was home to many Vietnamese American-owned businesses. In 2005, one of the barbers in the strip mall's salon was trying to gain U.S. citizenship. Unfortunately, he kept failing the test. The primary reason was he could not pronounce the name of William Rehnquist, who was Chief Justice for 19 years. His last name is extremely difficult for Vietnamese Americans to say with our natural accents. (Even with my best effort it still comes out sounding like "WRECK-ist" when I say it.) However,

William Rehnquist had just passed away and John Roberts was the new Chief Justice. I asked the barber to repeat after me: "John Roberts." He said that name with much greater ease. I told him this was the new Chief Justice of the U.S. Supreme Court. He took the exam again and finally passed it, which was a huge honor for him and his family. He was able to sponsor his wife as a migrant and they were reunited after a long time apart.

When I became friendly enough with Chief Justice Roberts, I told him that story.

"I bet you didn't realize your name would allow somebody to get citizenship and reunite with his wife from another country," I said.

He looked at me and thought I was joking. I told him that if I wanted to tell a joke, I would not do that to the Chief Justice. Then, we laughed together.

I got to know Chief Justice Roberts' assistant. One day, he told me that I could watch the proceedings of a Supreme Court case anytime I wanted. There was no way I wasn't taking him up on that offer! He told me to just check the Supreme Court's calendar on the Court's website and pick the case of my choice.

I selected one and when Chief Justice Roberts heard I was coming, he told his assistant to usher me into the building a bit early so I could see his chambers — another offer I couldn't refuse. During my visit, I saw the table where the nine justices convene to decide a case, adjacent to Chief Justice Roberts' office. I learned from Chief Justice Roberts that when the justices meet under such conditions, no one else is allowed in the chamber besides the nine of them. If one of the justices needs something, like a pen or a bottle of water, the justice with the least seniority has to run that errand.

I also saw the justices' dining room; the robing room, which is where the justices store their robes; and the second bathroom for women justices, only built in 1993 when the Court welcomed its second female member, Ruth Bader Ginsburg. I also walked onto the building's basketball court, which is located one floor above the courtroom. Justice Byron White, a former basketball player, once made the joke that the basketball court is technically the highest court in the land, not the Supreme Court.

After the visit to the Chief Justice's chamber, I was escorted to the courtroom where I was seated at a bench to the left of the justices. There is a tag on that bench that reads: "Guests of the Chief Justice." I bet most of the people in the court that day were wondering who was that Asian guy sitting at the Chief Justice's bench. At 10:00 a.m. sharp the curtain opened, and out walked the nice justices of the U.S. Supreme Court. It was so impressive, even though I probably understood about a quarter of what was going on. Nonetheless, I was the guest of the Chief Justice, which was what mattered most to me.

\* \* \*

By 2010, I'd counted eight of the nine sitting Supreme Court Justices as customers of mine, having photographic proof of this, too. (I'd even been invited to the Supreme Court Christmas Party!) The only holdout was Justice Ruth Bader Ginsberg. But then the National Asian Pacific American Bar Association, an organization that supports Asian American lawyers, coordinated an event in which she would be the guest of honor and give the keynote speech. Myself and personnel from Meiwah catered the event, setting up a buffet. I waited for the right moment to approach Justice Ginsberg when she walked from the Conference room to the dining room where we set up the food stand.

When I did, I introduced myself and said, "You know, I have a picture with almost all of the sitting Supreme Court Justices. I'm only missing one."

"Which one don't you have a picture with?" she asked.

"You," I said.

I'd been told that she doesn't like having her picture taken, but she made an exception for me.

I'd also been told that she didn't eat much, which made sense given her diminutive frame. When it came time to serve the food, she was first in line. I was there, ready to put whatever she wanted on her plate, while mindfully keeping the portions small. But when I placed a tiny helping of the first dish on her plate she asked for more. By the time she reached the end of the buffet, her plate was almost overflowing. I offered to carry it to her table for her, which she accepted.

By the end of the meal, her plate was empty, which I took as a great compliment!

After that event, I was very proud to have had pictures taken with each of the nine Justices of the U.S. Supreme Court at the time. (With Amy Barrett and Ketanji Brown Jackson having replaced two of the nine I'd met, my photo collection is technically incomplete again, but I'm trying my best to change that.)

A few years after first meeting Justice Ginsburg, Meiwah hosted a post-wedding dinner one day after her grandson was married. That was arranged through a friend of mine, Thao Griffiths, who's also a friend of Justice Ginsburg's daughter, Jane. It was an honor to host the Ginsburg family, and even though Meiwah was closed on Sundays at that time, I opened the restaurant just for them — of course I did.

Upon her death, Justice Ginsburg was honored in a ceremony in Statuary Hall, and she became the first woman to lie in state at the Capitol, on September 25, 2020. I was so honored to attend the ceremony and pay my respects to her.

\* \* \*

Famous people continued to show up to Meiwah through the years, which helped me and my business partners open a second location in Chevy Chase, the town in Maryland. JBG Smith, a real estate investment company, decided in 2002 that they wanted to build a new headquarters in a high-rise office building along with another two-story retail building. Their representatives asked us to put a new Meiwah inside the retail building and we agreed. It was good timing because after 9/11 there were far fewer travelers coming in and out of D.C., which was hurting Meiwah's bottom line. Meiwah would occupy the whole second floor. Many of my peers in the hospitality industry advised me not to operate a restaurant on the second floor. I thought to myself that I had run a restaurant in the basement before, City Lights of China; then, I opened Meiwah on the street level. Now I wanted to try the second floor.

It worked out just fine.

Like the first Meiwah, it took us about a year to build a second one. It seated 150 people in the dining room and another 50 on the patio. The rent was lower on the second floor than it would have been on the first floor, and a lot of our orders went out for delivery, so it didn't really matter what floor we were on. Many people who work in Washington D.C. also live in Chevy Chase and nearby Bethesda, so we ended up serving many of the same customers at home in the evening instead of during their lunch hour or post-work dinnertime.

In Chevy Chase, shortly after we opened we served Supreme Court Justice Sonia Sotomayor, which was such an honor. We were off to a good start yet again. In this location, we also served the World Bank President, Dr. Jim Yong Kim; the former Secretary of Defense, William Cohen; Senator Chris Van Hollen; Congressperson Jamie Raskin and his wife, Sarah Bloom Raskin; the Deputy Secretary of Treasury under President Obama, Senator Ben Cardin; and Maryland Governors Bob Ehrlich, Martin O'Malley and Larry Hogan to name a few high-profile guests.

We also served another Governor of Maryland, Robert Ehrlich. In fact, some Asian American community organizers held a rally at Meiwah for his re-election bid in 2007. It was standing-room-only, with about 250 guests. Elaine Chao, the Secretary of Labor, was the key-note speaker.

The security detail for Governor Ehrlich told me that they needed a place to put him and Secretary Chao before joining the rally in the dining room.

I said, "Sir, this is a restaurant. We do not have a place like that."

"Find one, please," he said.

I ended up cleaning my small office to have it ready to receive the Governor and the Secretary. I felt bad that they had to jam themselves into such a small space, but that was the best I could do. (I'm not sure if they used my office phone, but they might have!)

When the programming started, there were so many people that I could not even see the speakers. Then I heard Governor Ehrlich say, "Where is Larry?" At that time, Mr. Larry Hogan, a cabinet member of the Ehrlich Administration, who later also became Governor of Maryland, raised his hand. Governor Ehrlich said, "No, not you. I want the other Larry." Everyone got out of my way so that I could get up front and stand between Governor Ehrlich and Secretary Chao. Then the Governor said, "I have never seen an office that small. It looks like a closet."

"Governor, restaurant owners do not make money to have a big office," I said. "If we did I'd need a bigger dining room."

Then, the Governor said, "What a true entrepreneur!" The whole room laughed.

\*\*\*

One time, in the D.C. Meiwah, I helped Art Buchwald, the *Washington Post* humor columnist, find his hearing aid on the floor. Service was very busy, but Mr. Buchwald was a prominent person in the city and a Meiwah regular. Plus, he'd helped write the story for the movie *Coming To America*, which Diana and I saw on our first date. I dashed to his side and helped him find the hearing aid.

Senator Tom Harkin, who served in the U.S. Navy during the Vietnam War, was another frequent guest. He brought me a very nice bottle of whiskey from his home state of Iowa. He was a great Senator. I wish he was still in office.

Even though I am from the State of Maryland, I got to know the former Senator from Louisiana very well. She and her family have been our loyal customers for many years during her three-terms as Senator. When Alisa was thirteen years old, Senator Landrieu offered her an opportunity to join the teens from her State of Louisiana for three days "Take your daughters to work with the Senator". When we got together with the kids and their parents before meeting Senator Landrieu, the teens asked each other what city they were from in Louisiana, Alisa was from the State of Maryland. They wondered why she was in the group.

We jokingly pointed out that our last name is LA, the abbreviation of the State of Louisiana. Everyone laughed about that. The teenagers spent three days with the Senator while she was working in the Senate, at the Press Conference, visiting the U.S. Supreme Court and other female Senators, even cooking dinner at home. What an experience that Alisa had.

At Meiwah I also got to know one of the U.S. Senators representing Hawaii, Daniel Akaka, who was so kind and one of my favorite Senators. He was very unassuming. I once attended a wedding reception at a big Chinese restaurant in Rosslyn, Virginia. I was friends with the restaurant's owner and his son was the man who got married. There were about 600 people at the reception, including many politicians. (I wasn't the only restaurant owner in D.C. who got to knock elbows with the nation's most powerful people.)

I spotted Senator Akaka at the table next to mine, with nobody paying much attention to him, even the folks sitting at the same table. I went over to show him a picture of the two of us at Meiwah DC taken a few years earlier. Pointing to himself, he jokingly said, "I recognize that young man."

We started talking and, soon, the M.C. for the wedding began calling out the names of some of the distinguished guests. But he failed to mention Senator Akaka.

I went to the restaurant owner and told him, "You know, you have a sitting Senator here and the M.C. didn't even mention him! It's Senator Akaka from Hawaii."

A few minutes later, the M.C. once again took to the microphone and said, "There's one more guest I'd like to acknowledge, the State Senator from Hawaii Daniel Akaka!"

In terms of government rank, there's a tremendous difference between a *State* Senator and a *U.S.* Senator. Mr. Akaka was a *U.S.* Senator, and I said to Senator Akaka, "I'm so sorry they announced your title incorrectly."

"Don't worry about it," he said, sincerely not minding at all. "It doesn't have anything to do with you."

Another Hawaiian Senator who also came to Meiwah was the late Senator Daniel Inouye. He later became the President pro tempore of the Senate, a job that came with a security detail. Twice a year, during the summer and winter, he would treat his security detail to dinner at Meiwah. Per protocol, one of the security guards had to remain outside the restaurant, but Senator Inouye never let it happen. He always had all the security personnel join the dinner, which I thought was very kind.

He invited them for dinner at Meiwah two weeks before he passed away. I was so honored to attend his funeral at the National Cathedral, where I listened to President Barack Obama deliver the eulogy.

As much as I liked Senator Akaka and Senator Inouye, my most favorite Senator was Frank Lautenberg, from New Jersey, who was a City Lights of China defector to Meiwah. The year he retired from the Senate, in 2000, he had a celebratory dinner party at Meiwah for about 20 people: friends, colleagues and members of his family. He said to me that night, "Larry, now that I'm retiring, I'm going to get myself a nice car. I've ordered me a red BMW."

As a sitting U.S. Senator, it was bad form to drive a foreign car — even though BMWs were actually manufactured in Alabama and Tennessee, while many American cars are actually made in Mexico.

Two years later, Mr. Lautenberg came out of retirement and ran for New Jersey Senator again, this time for the junior seat. Senator Robert Toricelli was in a re-election campaign during the midterms, but eventually became the subject of federal corruption charges, which led to his withdrawal. The Democratic Party called up Mr. Lautenberg, who was still very popular in the state, and asked him to run. Not only did he run, he won, and found himself back in Washington D.C.

When I saw him at Meiwah after his election, I asked him, "So, Senator, now that you're out of retirement, are you going to sell your red BMW to me?"

He had no recollection of telling me he was going to buy one. "How did you know I had a red BMW?" he asked.

"Don't worry about that," I said. "I just want to know if you'll sell it to me."

"No," he said. "That's staying in my garage."

We shared a big laugh.

For one reason or another Senator Lautenberg's wife continued to live in New Jersey. He would go visit her often, but when he had to be in Washington D.C., he lived at the Ritz Carlton Residence, located across from Meiwah. He'd come to the restaurant often, mostly by himself, and he'd invite me to sit and talk to him, which was a kind gesture. We'd talk about the Senate and all kinds of political goings on in America and around the world. He was so impressed with my insights that one time he said, "You know more about politics than some of my staff."

I said, "Well, I just watch the news on TV and read a lot, too."

Then, off the cuff he said, "How about I give you a part-time job in my office?"

I was blown away by that offer. I'm not exactly sure what he thought I would do, but I guess he figured I'd be helpful. I thanked him profusely, but I turned down the gig. "I'm sorry, but I have two restaurants to run; I don't have time," I said.

I feel so honored I got to sit with Senator Lautenberg and talk to him so many times. Another interesting moment involving Senator Lautenberg that took place at my restaurant was when aides for Senators Harry Reid and Hillary Clinton asked me to bring "an exotic drink" to Mr. Lautenberg's table. He was sitting by himself over dinner and they wanted to have some fun with him. My waitress brought over a Hawaiian-style cocktail called the Volcano. It has Bacardi 151 rum in it that gets lit on fire.

"Where'd this come from?" he asked.

Senator Lautenberg was well into his 80s at that point — though you wouldn't have known it because he was so energetic. One time, he saw my daughter Alisa, who was still working as a page in the Senate, hanging out with a bunch of colleagues. He recognized her and when he passed by he started chanting, "Mei-wah! Mei-wah! Mei-wah!" Everyone chanted along. It was hilarious and I think a bit embarrassing for Alisa. After he asked where the Volcano drink came from, I said to him, pointing in the direction of the Reid and Clinton aides, "Those young people over there just wanted to say hello."

Before you knew it, he went over to their table with his drink and sat down with them. A few minutes later there was a lot of noise and laughing. They wound up having a really good time. I overheard Senator Lautenberg tell the staffers, "Whatever conversation we have today, it is *off the record!*"

\* \* \*

There were other very kind politicians I met as a restaurateur, including Ray LaHood, from Illinois, who was in the Republican House of Representatives while I ran both City Lights of China and

Meiwah. But then in 2009, President Barack Obama appointed him Secretary of Transportation, the only Republican in an otherwise Democratic administration. One perk that comes with the Secretary of Transportation job is that you have a personal driver and security guard. One night Secretary LaHood came into Meiwah alone and I said, "Where's your driver?"

"I don't like to have him take me to restaurants," he told me. "Then he'd have to just sit around and wait for me in the car. I don't feel comfortable eating like that."

"But that's his job," I said.

"I tricked him," Mr. LaHood said. He explained that, when the driver dropped him off at his home, he told him he wouldn't need his services anymore that night. "A few minutes later, I left home and walked here by myself."

I thought that was an interesting arrangement from a sitting U.S. Secretary of Transportation. He was such a great and kind gentleman.

One night when I was talking to him at Meiwah, Mr. LaHood asked me to go to his office and have lunch with him, which was really exciting and humbling. A few days later, the Secretary's scheduler called me and gave me a list of three days that Mr. LaHood was available.

"Any day is good for me," I said. I picked the first available one.

We set it up and the day of the lunch I arrived early to the Department of Transportation's building in Southeast Washington D.C. — extra early because I certainly didn't want to be late. Mr. LaHood was in a meeting, so I spoke with his secretary a little bit. It turned out that she had worked for many other Secretaries of Transportation in the past, and she presumed I was someone important.

"What state do you serve as Congressman?" she asked me at one point.

"Oh, no, I'm no Congressman," I said. "I just run a restaurant."

We both started laughing.

When Secretary LaHood was finished with his meeting, he welcomed me into his huge office, and he asked a photographer who worked for the Department of Transportation to take a picture of the two of us together. Then we went into the executive dining room, which was primarily reserved for the Secretary and high-level officers at the Department. All the people who worked there greeted me and were very kind. But based on what Secretary LaHood's secretary said to me, I always wondered if the people who served me that day thought I was some ambassador from Vietnam, China or Korea, perhaps.

Secretary LaHood and I had a wonderful time together, and four years later when he decided to leave government service and enter the private sector, I sent him an email saying that since he was leaving office we should have lunch again. He agreed. What an honor to have lunch with the Secretary of Transportation in his office twice.

He's no longer living in Washington D.C. but is still a customer of mine, one of the best and nicest.

As a refugee from Vietnam, I am also very proud to have known the two Vietnamese Americans who've been elected to the U.S. House of Representatives: Joseph Cao from Louisiana and Stephanie Murphy from Florida who served three terms in Congress.

I am also so proud to know Admiral Huan Nguyen, the only Vietnamese American to be promoted to Rear Admiral in the U.S. Navy. I got so friendly with him that I was invited to his retirement ceremony at the Navy Yard.

Besides politicians, judges and other notable figures closely associated with our Nation's Capital, I've also met a few famous professional athletes, including two Dallas Cowboys, Dat Nguyen and Emmitt

Smith and basketball players Chris Bosh, of Miami Heat, and Roger Mason and John Wall, who both played for the Washington Wizards.

Perhaps the most incredible athlete I've met was Sun Mingming, a gentleman from China who stood 7 feet, 9 inches. He also played basketball, as a member of the Maryland Nighthawks, a team in the American Basketball Association, which is a semi-professional minor league to the National Basketball Association.

Mingming is the tallest player in professional basketball history. When the Nighthawks introduced him at a national press conference, it was held at Meiwah. I was asked to be his interpreter. At five-foot-six, my face didn't even reach his chest. The Associated Press photographer assigned to the press conference took a picture of the two of us, and it was transmitted all over the world. The photographer asked me how tall I was so she could include the height disparity between Mingming and myself in the photo's caption.

The very next day, I took a train to Downtown D.C. and grabbed a newspaper, *The Express*, at the station. A rider sitting next to me was also reading *The Express*, and at one point I heard him say, "Wow!" I looked over and saw that he was looking at the AP photo of Mingming and me. I tapped his shoulder and said: "Sir, the short guy is me." He looked at me, said "wow" again and asked where the picture was taken. It turned out to be an opportunity to introduce Meiwah to a new customer. How many times are you in public transportation looking at the picture in the newspaper and the person in the picture just happens to sit next to you. It was a very rare and interesting situation.

\* \* \*

In 2004, I got to go to the Republican National Convention in New York City. Once again, a customer connection led to this privilege. All the hotels in New York were booked, but fortunately I have a friend in New York who was kind enough to open their home to me. It was great fun.

One of the reasons I wanted to go to the event was because on more than one occasion people complained to me that the D.C. Meiwah restaurant's Wall of Fame had pictures of many more Democrats than Republicans. (Someone actually took the time to count the number of Democrats and Republicans on the walls!) I always told them that if they knew any Republicans that like Chinese food, please bring them to Meiwah. I would love to take a picture with them for our restaurant's Wall of Fame. As a restaurant owner, I don't favor one side of the aisle or the other. I just favor my customers! But even though it was completely unintentional, I could understand why some people might think we were expressing favoritism with our selections to the Wall of Fame. So, I decided to go to the RNC Convention. Where else could you find so many Republicans in one place?

At the RNC I had pictures taken with many prominent Republican leaders and supporters: U.S. Senator from North Carolina Elizabeth Dole, Governor of Alabama Bob Riley, syndicated columnist Cal Thomas, former Speaker of the House Newt Gingrich, Speaker of the House Dennis Hastert and many others. I had a near all-access credential and I made good use of it. After that special occasion, I had many Republican pictures on our Meiwah Wall of Fame. Now everyone is happy.

Actually, a reporter from the *New York Post* who I was friendly with asked me at the convention how I was able to get my impressive credential. I told him, "I won't reveal my source." He liked that one.

In 2014, I was interviewed by the famous journalist Elizabeth Williamson of the *Wall Street Journal* about the Meiwah "Wall of Fame." She was writing an article about some famous "Me Walls" — where folks post pictures of themselves with different famous people — in the city. Mine made the cut.

"More than 600 portraits of Mr. La grin from the walls in a gallery that is the essence of democracy," Williamson wrote. "Mr. La's captioned portrait with Department of Homeland Security Deputy Secretary Alejandro Mayorkas shares the same chunk of plywood paneling as one captioned 'Mr. Ronnie Wood, the Rolling Stone.'"

Not everybody loved the Meiwah Wall of Fame and displeasure with it extended beyond the perceived partisan nature of the photo collection. In the early 2000s I received a very harsh email from one customer who wrote, "Since you support a lying, election law breaking moron ... I pray for your restaurant to suffer, lose customers, and go out of business." It didn't matter which politician he was referencing. Everyone on the Wall of Fame ate at Meiwah, which was meaningful to me. I wrote back to him:

*Meiwah opened business to the general public. We are not in the business of supporting or opposing any person regardless of his or her political beliefs. We welcome everyone who walks into our doors. I myself escaped from a Communist country. Having said that, if any Communist Group wants to have any event at Meiwah, we will be more than happy to accept their reservation. The world is chaotic enough. Why don't you and I say prayers for the good things?*

I then asked him to come to the restaurant to have a drink with me and talk the issue over. I never heard back from him, but every year I send him holiday greetings emails.

\*\*\*

I also served Senator Lamar Alexander, who represented Tennessee between the years 2003 and 2021. He was Governor of the state when I worked for the Clinchfield Railroad Company. He even visited Erwin once, and a coworker of mine took him to a mountain in the Appalachians to see the many ginseng roots that made it locally famous. While Governor, he also spoke at East Tennessee State University during my graduation ceremony. When he became Secretary of Education under President George H.W. Bush in the early 1990s, he and his wife visited City Lights of China. When the then Secretary walked in, I recognized him right away.

"Oh, Governor," I said, referencing his time serving Tennessee. "Great to see you here."

He just said to me, "Who's Larry?"

"Me," I said.

"So, you're the Larry from Tennessee they're talking about," Mr. Alexander said.

"Yes, sir," I said.

He explained that the U.S. Attorney General at the time, Dick Thornburgh, told him that a guy from Tennessee named Larry runs the best Chinese restaurant in town.

"How in the world can a guy from Tennessee run a Chinese restaurant in Washington D.C.?" Mr. Alexander asked me.

We laughed and then I told him my story. At the end of his meal, I approached him and his wife with a special bottle of Chinese plum wine.

I said, "Secretary, I'd like to offer you some Chinese moonshine."

He said, "Oh, you know about moonshine, eh?"

"Yes, sir," I said. "I'm from East Tennessee."

When I mention that, people often say to me in surprise, "Really, you're from Tennessee?"

I say, "Yep, I just lost my accent, but I have my Tennessee moonshine to prove it."

* * *

In 2006, I was invited to the White House Christmas Party, hosted by President George W. Bush. I brought my daughter Alisa with me, and we met the President and the First Lady, Laura. The photo opportunity was only supposed to last a few seconds. If everyone at the party stopped to chat with the two of them for a couple minutes they would have remained in that spot overnight.

There was a U.S. Marine standing close by and I got the sense that if anyone went against protocol he would drag them away. But I also had a feeling the President and the First Lady would make a slight exception for me. They had both been in Vietnam a few months earlier for an Asian-Pacific Economic Cooperation summit. Their four-day visit was just the second trip to Vietnam by a sitting U.S. President.

After my picture with the President and First Lady was snapped, I turned around and said, "You know, Mr. President, I'm from Vietnam." They seemed happy to talk about the country and we wound up speaking for a few minutes. President Bush said to me, "You should visit Vietnam; there are a lot of business opportunities there," to which I replied, "Mr. President, we have a lot of business opportunities here in this great country, too!" He said, "Well yes, you're right about that."

Being invited to Christmas Parties thrown by the D.C. elite became old hat for me as time went on. In 2011, White House Chief of Staff Pete Rouse got me an invitation to President Barack Obama's annual gathering. Both of his daughters, Malia and Sasha, were customers of mine at Meiwah, in both locations, actually. They'd come for dinner with their friends many times and I said hello to them.

I remember one night I walked out to check on the dining room and I spotted Malia with her friends at the corner table. I knew that she had just come back from a visit to China with the First Lady, Michelle Obama, as well as her sister and her grandmother, Marian Shields Robinson. They were invited by Madame Peng Liyuan, wife of the President of China Xi Jinping. I felt good that Malia was at Meiwah, still enjoying our food after spending six days eating in Beijing, Xi'an and Chengdu.

Whenever she and her sister Sasha came to Meiwah I made sure not to mention the President or his wife, Michelle, the First Lady. I didn't want to come off as too eager. But on one occasion, after I got to know them a little bit, I couldn't resist. Sasha came to Meiwah's Washington D.C. restaurant with her friends and her grandmother. I asked Sasha what her favorite dishes at Meiwah were and she said wonton soup and orange chicken. With the ice broken, I casually said, "You know, you should bring in your parents sometime."

Sure enough, a week later I got a call from the Secret Service who told me that Michelle Obama wanted to dine at Meiwah in the upstairs dining room. You can imagine how exhilarated I was to hear that. My staff was, too.

We had two entrances, and the one on the side, which we used for carryout service, was locked down the night of her visit. In the front, every guest was checked in by the Secret Service, almost all of whom were *not* in the First Lady's party, which numbered about 20. Normally, people would be upset that their dinner was being delayed, and that they were being scanned with electronic wands by security guards at a restaurant. Not this time though. After being shocked that the First

Lady was there and the discomfort over being checked by the Secret Service wore off, everyone was excited. I still apologized for the inconvenience and one family of tourists from England said, "No, no, no. This is the highlight of our trip to Washington D.C., getting to see the First Lady come to a Chinese Restaurant with all this security and everything. It's incredible!"

Mrs. Obama ordered a lot of food for her party. I assigned two waitresses just to the upstairs dining room. A good time was had by all, including me, who had a little laugh at the expense of a Secret Service agent. One of them was stationed next to the kitchen to watch the back entrance. But all of Mrs. Obama's food was being run past him and as a goof I said, "Sir, will you be tasting all of the food as it comes out of the kitchen?" I was referencing how in olden times, the Emperors or Empresses of China had food tasters in case their dishes were poisoned. The Secret Service agent at first looked at me like I was crazy. I had to explain to him what I meant. He eventually got it, smiled and shook his head. Secret Service agents sure are tough to break!

When I got to go to the Obama White House Christmas Party, I felt very comfortable, having gotten so chummy with Malia and Sasha, plus their mother and grandmother. Like the photo opportunity at the Bush White House party, this year's was only supposed to last a few seconds. But after my picture with the President and First Lady was snapped, Mrs. Obama told the President that I was from Meiwah and Malia and Sasha were our regulars. The President said, "I should visit Meiwah then." I replied, "Anytime, Mr. President. It will be our honor."

One time in May, the Asian American Heritage Month, the White House had an event to celebrate the occasion. I managed to present my business card to President Obama. I told him that if he could not find Pete Rouse, his senior advisor, in the White House, call that restaurant's number. The President smiled and held the business card up and said, "Now I know where to find Pete." Everyone at the event laughed and was shocked that I gave my business card to the President of the United States. I really wish he'd used it, but, for now, I'll be happy knowing I served his family.

They weren't the last members of a Presidential family I served. When Mr. Joe Biden was Vice President, I took a call at the take-out department at Meiwah. When I put the phone number into the system, I saw the name "Biden." After I finished taking the order, I asked the young lady on the phone whether she knows Joe Biden. "That is my grandfather," she replied.

After Joe Biden entered the White House, he became the first President to celebrate the Lunar New Year, in January 2023. A party was thrown in the East Wing with lion dancing. I was invited and gave President Biden my Meiwah business card. While he held the card up, I said, "Mr. President, in case you don't know, your granddaughter is a Meiwah customer."

* * *

Another iconic D.C. building to which I was granted access was the Pentagon. I went there twice with Meiwah staff to cater events. On both occasions, the U.S. Secretary of Defense under President Obama — first Leon Panetta, in 2012, and then Chuck Hagel, the next year — hosted the National Defense Minister of China and other delegates. The National Defense Minister in 2012 was General Liang Guanglie, and the one in 2013 was General Chang Wanquan. My Meiwah cooking staff actually got to prepare the meal in the Pentagon kitchen! It was quite an honor, and a challenge. The kitchen was huge, at least twice the size of the one we had at Meiwah. But the burners in the Pentagon's kitchen didn't deliver heat in the same way that ours at Meiwah did. To compensate, we cooked some of the food partway at Meiwah and finished it off at the Pentagon.

Prior to the 2012 event, I was at the Pentagon to check out their kitchen. I was able to tour the E Ring of the Pentagon, which is the outermost rotunda where senior officers — like the Joint Chiefs of Staff, the Secretary of the Army — and planning staff do their business. Secretary of Defense Leon Panetta's Chief of Staff, who at that time was Jeremy Bash, was a good customer and good friend. I'd first gotten to know him just after he graduated college. He said hi to me at the Pentagon and said that Secretary Panetta was on his way from his office. I was honored to meet Mr. Panetta, who was very friendly and unabashedly asked me, "So what kind of drinks are you serving tomorrow?" I said, "Moonshine." He laughed and said, "No, no, we can't do that." We wound up serving wine that originated in the state Mr. Panetta was from: California.

I was also invited to the State Department for lunches and dinners where I saw so many dignitaries. In 2011, I saw Mr. Xi Jinping, who at the time was Vice President of China, but later became the country's President — which prompted a return to the U.S. State Department for another event that I also attended. Even better, for me at least, I got to meet the President of Vietnam, Trương Tấn Sang. He and I were having a very pleasant conversation when over walked Secretary of State John Kerry. President Tấn Sang wound up introducing me to Secretary Kerry, who famously served in the Vietnam War, saying, "This gentleman is from the Mekong Delta, where I'm from." I also got to meet the Prime Minister of Singapore, Lee Hsien Loong, the son of the Legendary PM Lee Kuan Yew, who was from the same town of Dapo as my father.

And through the years I was also invited to many embassies where my staff and I catered different events. The embassies I've visited include those of Ireland, France, Russia, and others tied to countries in Asia, such as Indonesia, Brunei, the Philippines, Myanmar, Laos, Cambodia, China, Malaysia and, yes, Vietnam, too. Every year at the Vietnam Embassy they have celebrations marking Tet, the Lunar New Year, and the country's independence day, which honors Vietnam's liberation from Japan and France at the end of World War II. I've attended many of those parties at the Vietnam embassy in D.C. In my mind, the fighting was over. No matter the victors, it was just nice to be around people from my country and bond with them, over food especially.

Having visited so many embassies, and having run restaurants within walking distance of a number of them, I've befriended many ambassadors. One of them was Ambassador Sebatane from the Kingdom of Lesotho, a landlocked country encircled by South Africa. In August 2014, when President Obama had a U.S.-Africa Summit, leaders from across the African continent were welcome to Washington D.C. One of these leaders was Prime Minister of the Kingdom of Lesotho, Tom Thabane, who was introduced to Meiwah by his country's Ambassador. He dined at Meiwah three times during his one-week stay in D.C. His last visit to Meiwah came right before he left the city for the airport. I asked him to autograph the picture that we took together a few days before. Two weeks later, there was "breaking news" on CNN. I saw the very same Prime Minister that I met only two weeks ago had fled to South Africa, alleging that the military was about to attempt a coup d'état and wanted to kill him. He returned to Lesotho a few days later under the protection of South African police. Fortunately, he continued to serve in office for a while and was never assassinated.

# SQUARE MOON

\* \* \*

There are countless more stories I have of waiting on the Washington elite.

Among the better ones, there was the time in 2006 when Pete Rouse, who was then Chief of Staff for the junior U.S. Senator from Illinois, Barack Obama, told me at Meiwah that Obama was thinking of running for President. Pete said that if Obama ran for the highest office in the land, he would help the campaign. A year later, that consideration turned into a full-blown campaign, and Mr. Rouse told me that if Obama won the White House he would no longer work for him. I guess he didn't want to live in that kind of pressure cooker anymore after 35 years on Capitol Hill, where he held many advisory positions. But when Obama won the election, there was Mr. Rouse in the White House, first as Senior Advisor, then Chief of Staff (the first-ever Asian American to fill that role), and finally Counselor to the President. I guess it's hard to refuse a request from the President of the United States of America! While Pete was in the White House, I got to be invited to have lunch at the famous White House Mess and also visited the Oval Office.

Secretary of Defense Robert Gates was in Meiwah one day in 2008, shortly after Obama won the Presidential election. There was a rumor going around that Obama was going to ask Secretary Gates to remain in that position even after President Bush, who'd appointed him, left office. After his meal at Meiwah with his wife and family, he cracked open a fortune cookie. I said, "Does the fortune cookie say if you will continue on as Secretary of Defense during the new administration?" He looked up and said, smiling, "I don't know." And then his wife said, "Do you have a tape recorder in your pocket?" I laughed; they did, too, and he wound up staying in the Obama cabinet and served as one of the best Secretaries of Defense in our nation's history, in my opinion at least.

I once spotted Robert Magnus at Meiwah. He was a four-star general, but there he was, in civilian clothes, having dinner.

"General," I said, approaching him. "How can I take a picture with you so people can tell you are a four-star general?"

The smile on my face indicated I was asking in a somewhat joking manner. He smiled back and replied, "Give me your email address. Let's see what we can do."

Two weeks later, I received an email from the General with the chain of command from the General down to the Staff Sergeant. In Southeast Washington D.C., there is a Marine Barracks that was established in 1801, the oldest post in the U.S. Marine Corps. It is a Historic Landmark and, since 1806, it's also been the official residence of the Commandant of the Marine Corps. During the summer, on the grounds is what's called the Friday Evening Parade, featuring performances by "The President's Own" United States Marine Band, "The Commandant's Own" United States Marine Drum and Bugle Corps, and the esteemed United States Marine Corps Silent Drill Platoon. Following the ceremony, guests have the opportunity to meet Marines who performed throughout the parade as well as take photographs.

The email recipients' list ran all the way down to the Staff Sergeant responsible for inviting guests to the General's reception in the garden yard of the residence of the Commandant. I was so thrilled to receive the invitation to attend the reception along with the Friday Evening Parade.

I replied immediately to the Staff Sergeant. The invitation called for just one guest, but I talked him into allowing me to bring two guests since I have two children. He kindly accepted my request, so I had both Alisa and Tim beside me at this special event.

We were so excited to arrive at the party. It turned out the reception held by General Magnus was to honor the retirement of the Secretary of Transportation, Mr. Norman Mineta, whom I got to know well when he was a Congressperson from San Jose, California. During the reception, we got to tour the residence of the Commandant of the Marine Corps. After the reception, we were escorted to the Marine Barracks' main ceremonial grounds to watch the United States Marine Corps Silent Drill Platoon. What an exciting experience for me and my kids.

Through my work as a restaurant owner, I also had the privilege to be a part of the FBI's Citizens Academy, a program that gives nominated citizens an inside look at what goes on in the bureau. I took a weekly course with some other entrepreneurs in the community and it was fascinating. We learned about counterterrorism intelligence and got to visit Quantico, the FBI's primary training facility, after we "graduated." There, even though I'd previously spent so much time in a war zone, I held a gun for the first time in my life.

Somewhat relatedly, Meiwah got its few minutes of Hollywood fame in a movie with Chris Cooper and Ryan Phillippe. Called *Breach*, it was released in 2007 and is about a real-life FBI agent who was spying for the Soviet Union and Russia. One of the film's producers was based in Toronto, Canada. She called me at my office and told me a little bit about the project.

It wasn't long before I stopped her and said, "Ma'am, when are you just going to go ahead and ask me if I want to star in your movie?"

She laughed and said, "Is that the call you've been waiting for?"

Jokingly I said it was, but I was more than happy to fulfill her actual request. She wanted us to provide the filmmakers a bunch of our carryout boxes to help give the film an air of authenticity. There's a scene in Ryan Phillippe's character's home dining room where the table is littered with Meiwah boxes, with the name of the restaurant purposely scrawled across them. It was a tremendous pleasure to see them on the screen.

I used to host a program on the local TV station WUSA9 once a month about Asian American issues. I got to invite guests and discuss different topics with them. I also did a show on WUSA9 about food to celebrate Lunar New Year. It was really fun and also great publicity for my Meiwah restaurant.

But as wonderful as all of those events were, few of them could compare to the day in 2006 when Meiwah was the setting for a most special occasion. Guy and Ruth Johnson from the First Baptist Church in Erwin, Tennessee — the church that sponsored my family's arrival to the United States after we'd spent more than a year in a Malaysian refugee camp — traveled to Washington D.C. to celebrate their 50th anniversary. We had a big party at Meiwah restaurant to celebrate the occasion. She brought some other members of the parish and old friends of mine. My mother and some other family members of mine were there, too. (Unfortunately, Dad had passed away by then.)

It was a beautiful reunion with the people of the First Baptist Church, just shy of 30 years after our first meeting. It was an honor to serve them all and pay back just a small amount of their generosity.

# CHAPTER 8

In all my time in Washington D.C. it was my dream to attend a Presidential State of the Union Address. My wish was finally granted in 2013, shortly after President Obama was elected to a second term in office. Secretary of Transportation Ray LaHood provided me a ticket, which was so generous of him.

Security at the Capitol Building was very tight with multiple checkpoints and guests had to surrender their phones so there could be no picture-taking. But Capitol Building security didn't have the manpower to escort every single guest directly to their seat, and some confusion ensued as I tried to find mine. Somebody in one corridor told me my seat was through a door that I'd find after making a right-hand turn. When I made that turn, though, there were three doors.

I picked the middle one. There were two ushers there checking my ticket and they weren't sure where my seat was, so they just said I could sit in a seat in the back row against the wall of the House Gallery. It turned out, I was in the First Lady's box with special guests of the White House! I looked down the row and I saw they were reserved with pieces of papers hung on the backrests with their names on them. I thought, "Oh no, I won't be here very long."

But even after a while nobody asked me to leave. Valerie Jarrett wound up sitting next to me after she checked the First Lady's box. She was a top advisor to President Obama, and I recognized her right away. I gave her my business card and struck up a conversation with her. "I'm a friend of Pete Rouse's," I told her. "Oh! I'll send him an email and tell him I'm sitting with you," she said. She opened up her smartphone — apparently some special guests *were* allowed to hold onto their phones — and she rattled off an email to Mr. Rouse, never inquiring why I was in the First Lady's box.

Later on, invited guests started coming in. I saw Mr. Tim Cook, the CEO of Apple, show up. So did a Marine who'd lost two legs and an arm in battle sitting right in front of me. I spoke to him and gave him the contact information for Senator Cleland, who'd also lost two legs and an arm in the Vietnam War. I'm not sure if they ever connected, but I hope they did.

Sitting right next to me was Desiline Victor. She had gained a bit of notoriety for being 102 years old and a Haitian immigrant who stood for more than six hours in the rain in Miami to vote for President Obama on Election Day in 2012. The President invited her and used her story as a jumping off point to address the unfortunate challenges many Americans face in casting votes. Ms. Victor was supposed to sit in the front row of the box, right behind the First Lady, but she didn't want to walk down the stairs to get there. She looked at many steps down, shook her head and wound up next to me in the back. I shook her hand telling her that I would like to get some longevity tips from her. Ms. Victor got to vote again in 2016 before she passed away at 106 in 2017.

The seats were filling up fast. There were three empty seats on my right. I was hoping that for some reason those people could not make it. Soon, three ladies took the three seats next to me. As soon as they settled in their seats, one of them told me that they needed one more. I looked to my left and there stood Jane Sullivan Roberts, wife of Supreme Court

Chief Justice John Roberts, whom I'd met at Meiwah before. I realized that I was sitting in her seat. I got up and offered her my seat. "I've been keeping it warm for you, Mrs. Roberts," I said. She seemed to recognize me and said, "Sorry to take your seat."

Out of seats, I went into the suite next door, but it was still a pretty great place to be that night. From my vantage point, I could see the President turn the pages of his speech while standing at his podium, and I could look out into the whole chamber. I only wished I could have a picture taken of me in the box.

I went home abuzz and very satisfied about seeing the President of the United States deliver a State of the Union Address in person. The next day, I went to Meiwah and a regular customer, Bernadette Passade Cisse, who was also a Haitian immigrant, came in and ordered take out. She actually worked for the United Nations High Commissioner for Refugees. She said, "Larry, you were at the State of the Union Address last night, right?" I said that I was. I thought maybe she saw me on TV, but that wasn't the case. After the speech at the State of the Union, she searched the internet for a photo of Desiline Victor. A credentialed photojournalist in the chamber snapped a picture of her, and there I was, right next to her.

So I got my picture at the State of the Union Address after all!

\* \* \*

There were a few more events I had the honor of being able to attend, awarded such a chance because of my fortunate status as a successful entrepreneur in Washington D.C.

Every year in April at the Washington Hilton Hotel, about 3,000 people attend the White House Correspondents' Dinner, an important event that celebrates the First Amendment awarding every American the right to free speech. Its most honorary guests are the journalists who cover the White House and proceeds from the event go to their White House Correspondents' Association. A regular customer of mine, Ed Henry, was an award-winning TV journalist on CNN and later Fox News, but in April 2013 he was President of the White House Correspondents' Association. He graciously invited me to the dinner, where I met many different people from the media world and that of D.C. politics — even more than I was used to at my restaurants.

I had no interest in eating. I was too excited, and if the kitchen was serving 3,000 people, the food probably wasn't going to be very good in the first place. Instead, I took advantage of this once-in-a-lifetime opportunity and went around and introduced myself to people. I shook hands and took pictures with the actors Kerry Washington, Nicole Kidman, John Legend and Michael Douglas, as well as the film director Steven Spielberg, who took the time to ask me some personal questions, like where I was from and what I did in my professional life. I was very impressed with him. There was Jacob Lew, Secretary of the Treasury; Chuck Todd, from NBC News; Scott Pelley, from CBS News; Bill O'Reilly and Juan Williams, also from Fox News.

I had a great time. What a spectacle.

I've also attended George Washington University's graduation ceremony a number of times, annually held at the National Mall. I received tickets because I was part of the school's Parents' Association Advisory Council. Typically at this event there are 20,000 attendees included among the graduates and their families. All of them get the inevitable privilege of hearing a well-known figure give a keynote commencement speech.

One year I was there, Mr. Tim Cook, the CEO of Apple, was the speaker. When he began his remarks, he said, "Please set your *iPhones* in silent mode or turn them off. If you do not own iPhones, please pass your phones to the aisle, someone will pick them up. We have the biggest recycling program of non-iPhones." They say a speech like that should always start with a joke, and he began with a banger.

A few months later, I was invited to the State Lunch at the State Department, honoring President Xi Jinping of China. When I got in the building's elevator, I spotted Mr. Cook right away. Projecting my voice, I said, "What an honor to be in the same elevator with Mr. Tim Cook!" He smiled and I managed to repeat what he said at the George Washington University graduation. He was so happy someone paid attention to his speech. Of course, I had a picture of us taken after we got out of the elevator.

When Barack Obama was President, the Chief of Protocol was a woman named Capricia Marshall. In addition to advising the President, Vice President and Secretary of State on matters of national and international protocol, they also held the rank of Ambassador and Assistant Secretary of State. Ambassador Marshall was very active in her role, and she organized so many events, including one that I enjoyed immensely: the Diplomatic Culinary Partnership, a State Department initiative that uses food to engage foreign dignitaries. Food is always a great thing to use to start conversation and make connections. That's what Meiwah was all about, and participating in the event when I was asked by a member of her staff was a no-brainer for me.

I was at the annual event a few times, starting in 2013. There were so many different cultures represented and I got to meet chefs from all over the world, including the personal chefs for the President of Italy and the King of Thailand. The White House's Executive Chef was another; there was also a chef who serves the Congress of China and I also met Vikram Sunderam, the famous chef behind Rasika, as well as Executive Chef Marc Murphy, famous for his New York Restaurant Landmarc and from his appearances on Food Network shows like *Chopped*.

It was so much fun to meet so many famous chefs.

I always dress well for the occasions. One time I wore a Chinese traditional dress, the "Zhong Shan Zhuang" style named after Dr. Sun Yat-Sen. It looks very formal. I noticed one lady at the State Department party looked at me and smiled. I smiled back and she approached me to shake my hand. She asked, "Are you an ambassador? From what country?" I shook her hand and replied, "I am Ambassador from Meiwah." She looked confused by not knowing where Meiwah was located in the world. I told her that Meiwah was at the corners of M Street and New Hampshire Avenue. I immediately gave her my business card and said, "I am sorry, ma'am. I am just joking with you. I am no Ambassador. Meiwah is my restaurant in town." We both laughed.

*President Clinton's Congressional picnic in 2000*

*Delivering food to President Clinton*

*Congresswoman Stephanie Murphy, Florida*

*Lang Lang at Meiwah*

*Sun Ming Ming 7'9" tall, Larry 5'6" short at Meiwah Chevy Chase*

*Chief Justice John Roberts*

*Meiwah Chevy Chase*

*Senator Mary Landrieu, Louisiana*

*Senator Frank Lautenberg, New Jersey*

*Transportation Secretary Ray LaHood*

*President Clinton and First Lady*

*President Bush and First Lady*

*President Obama and First Lady*

*President Joe Biden*

*General Liang and Secretary Panetta*

*In the Pentagon kitchen with the chef and his crew*

# CHAPTER 9

In 2005, I experienced a full-circle moment — at least in my life as an American. At Meiwah's D.C. location, I'd met a man named Jim Rogers, who was President of the Southern Association of Colleges and Schools, an organization that included the college from which I graduated back in December 1984, East Tennessee State University. I told Mr. Rogers I'd attended the school and he said he'd alert its President that I was thriving as a restaurant owner.

A couple weeks later, I received a call from the school's alumni association, saying they wanted to interview me for the group's quarterly publication. They printed a nice article about me in the magazine, chronicling my success since graduation. The alumni association then asked me to sit on its board. I was so honored by that, and I began my yearly visits for important meetings with the board members, attending some others by phone. But when I'd drive out to East Tennessee State I'd always make a pit stop in my hometown of Erwin. I'd see many of the people from the First Baptist Church and colleagues from the old Clinchfield Railroad company — one of whom is still my moonshine connection.

Sitting on the alumni association's board wasn't the only honor my alma mater bestowed upon me. In 2010, the school's College of Business and Technology granted me a lifetime achievement award. I brought my wife and my kids to the university. It was their first time visiting Tennessee.

The school told me I could invite as many friends as I wanted to, but I'm not sure they realized quite how many I had. I invited so many people from Erwin, all the church members who helped me survive in my first years in this country. My guests took up three whole tables of space.

I was able to give a speech at the ceremony and I got pretty emotional calling out the names of the people who helped me, like John Keesecker, who donated the apartment where my family and I lived; Barbara Ollis, who lent me her Trans Am so I could take my first driver's license test; Ruth Johnson, who gave me $20 for postage stamps so that I could mail all the letters from my fellow refugees; and on and on.

I have the award hanging in my office today. It says, "Lifetime Achievement Award: Presented to Larry La in recognition of personal achievement and lifelong commitment to East Tennessee State University and the College of Business and Technology." A picture of me is also on the wall of the ETSU College of Business and Technology Wall of Fame. My face is the only one that's Asian American.

I also received the Golden Lantern Award, an honor bestowed upon people by the Chinese American Museum in D.C. for "their excellence, leadership, and service to the Chinese American community and beyond" — to quote the museum's website. It was another humbling moment, as I accepted the award at the exalted Kennedy Center.

In the event's program, the museum highlighted not just my community contributions via the Meiwah Restaurant Group, but also my work as Founder, Partner and VP Business Development of the U.S.-Asia Links organization, where, to put it briefly, we provide business development and management guidance to entrepreneurs and other business leaders around the world. Through this work we hope to enhance international relations. The museum also recognized me as a founding member of the Asian Pacific American Chamber of Commerce, a D.C.-based not-for-profit resource for Asian American businesses and businesspeople, helping them succeed.

Whatever help, insights and guidance I've been able to offer members of these groups — and others — only became valuable because the United States embraced an ambitious refugee some decades ago. It's been my pleasure, and honor, to give back in such ways.

*   *   *

Another Meiwah regular for whom it was a distinct pleasure to serve was Jeh Johnson, who became Secretary of Homeland Security during the Obama administration. I got to know Mr. Johnson first when he was working at the Department of Defense during Obama's first term. One time, Secretary Johnson's office organized a dinner reception at Meiwah for Mr. Guo Shengkun, the Minister of Public Security, China's top policeman, the counterpart of our Secretary of Homeland Security. Attorney General Loretta Lynch, the Deputy Director of the FBI, was in attendance, so you have a sense of the level of officials at the place. Each of them, from China and the U.S., had their own security detail. It seemed like there were more security guards than estimable guests! Meiwah was the safest space in all of Washington D.C. for that one night, which is really saying something.

I attended another event hosted by Mr. António Guterres, who was then the U.N. High Commissioner for Refugees, and now the U.N. Secretary-General. He was also a Meiwah customer. At that gathering, I met the former Director of the United States Citizen and Immigration Services, Mr. Alejandro Mayorkas, who later was serving in the Obama cabinet as the Deputy Secretary of Homeland Security. (Later he'd fill the role of Secretary of Homeland Security in the Biden Administration.) He spoke that night and I approached him after his keynote address, handing him my business card.

He looked at me and said, "You are the owner of Meiwah restaurant. I will tell my wife and my kids that I met you tonight." He made me feel like I was important.

It turned out that Mayorkas family had been Meiwah regulars, stopping by to pick up carryout on the way home. I was so honored to get to know such a gentleman.

Given his position in the government, I'm fairly certain it was he who recommended me for the Outstanding Americans by Choice award in 2015. What's also called the ABC award, it is an honor that recognizes a migrant's commitment to the U.S., exhibited by their civic participation, professional achievement and responsible citizenship. Only about six or seven people are honored in such a way each year by U.S. Citizenship and Immigration Services. When one of their representatives called me, I happened to be at that State Department luncheon where Xi Jinping was the guest of honor. My cell phone buzzed and flashed a phone number I didn't recognize. I picked up and quickly said that I couldn't talk at that moment. The woman on the other line said I could call back afterward, but she also identified herself as someone from U.S. Citizenship and Immigration Services. I had no idea why they wanted to get in touch with me and I thought something was wrong. I got a little nervous.

But when I arrived at my office a little while later and called her back, she explained that I was nominated for the Outstanding Americans by Choice award. I didn't realize how extraordinary the honor was until she sent me a detailed email. Past recipients were highly esteemed people, including former U.S. Secretary of Labor Elaine Chao, former Secretary of State Madeleine Albright, Nobel Peace Prize-winning author Elie Wiesel, and Deputy Secretary of Homeland Security/Meiwah regular Alejandro Mayorkas.

When I got back on the phone with the woman from U.S. Citizenship and Immigration Services I told her I thought she had the wrong guy. She laughed and said, "No, we don't choose you; you are nominated by somebody." She never told me who, but explained that the department had to sort of investigate me and get a full picture of my life and my work.

I guess they found what they were looking for because I went from an ABC award nominee to ABC award recipient. The ceremony was very formal. What made the award feel like an even greater honor to me was the lady with whom I was receiving it alongside that year, Maria Contreras-Sweet, who was born in Mexico and became an Obama cabinet member as Administrator of the U.S. Small Business Administration. A very famous baseball player, Mariano Rivera, who was born in Panama and later became a noted philanthropist, was also honored the same year as me.

I gave a speech, this one in front of about 400 people, including family and friends of the award recipients and other government officials, as well as 100 newly sworn-in American citizens and their families and friends. While making the speech, it brought tears to my eyes and a smile to my face. Many similar precious memories fluttered through my head as I was speaking. It was such an incredible honor.

Like the others given the ABC award, the certificate I received was signed by the current Director of the U.S. Citizenship and Immigration Services, León Rodríguez. I asked Deputy Secretary of Homeland Security Alejandro Mayorkas to sign it, too. A few weeks later, Secretary of

Homeland Security Jeh Johnson ordered a dinner for pickup from Meiwah. When he came in I asked him to sign it as well. So not one, not two, but *three* people from the Department of Homeland Security — the three most important ones — signed my ABC award.

Then, a few months later, Meiwah regular Marjorie O'Connor, a big-time lawyer in town, heard about my award and went to speak to Congressperson Chris Van Hollen, from Maryland. Apparently, a new American flag flies over the Capitol Building each day, and Ms. Connor believed Congressperson Van Hollen might be open to dedicating one of them to me, in recognition of my ABC award. Congressperson Van Hollen — who's now a Senator — kindly did so. The flag arrived with a letter signed by the Congressperson and a certificate from the Architect of the Capitol confirming that it flew over the Capitol on June 7, 2016. I've since spoken to Congressperson Van Hollen and he told me he was proud to see an immigrant resident of Maryland, the state he represents in the government, receive the ABC award.

All this appreciation heaped upon me by top leaders of the greatest country in the world… Considering where I came from, it truly is unbelievable. I just wanted to be an American — free to pursue my own version of happiness — like everyone else in the United States.

# EPILOGUE

It's March 2024, and I'm in Vietnam once again. This is my third time visiting my birthplace after leaving the country 46 years earlier. These days, it's much more pleasant than it was when I was a boy, I must say.

I'm having a wonderful time in the company of my college classmates, who I haven't seen in five decades. It's a big gathering, at a restaurant, and it's quite moving. The emotions are understandable considering the circumstances responsible for our lengthy time apart — circumstances that in any number of ways created challenging misfortune for so many people, including me. Though in my case, they also opened the possibilities for unlimited achievement.

After Vietnam, I make a special trip to Malaysia to meet Madame Ann, who worked for the Malaysian Red Crescent and was nearly instrumental in my ability to thrive at the camp. I can't believe I'm about to reconnect with her after 45 years.

Back in D.C., I met Mr. Sac Taufik Toh, who is Chief of the Special Branch law enforcement agency in Kuching, Sarawak. Before being promoted to that position, he was an officer at the Malaysian embassy in Washington and we became friends. Police Chief Toh picks me up at the Kuching Airport and takes me to the restaurant where his family is waiting for us for dinner. I'd texted Mr. Toh Madame Ann's name and hoped he could find her in that city. Within one day, he located her and visited her at her home to make sure she was the person I was looking for.

The day after I had dinner with the Toh family, I met with Madame Ann. She just turned 76 years old. We had lunch and reminisced at her home. What an emotional reunion after 45 years.

We speak about the Vietnamese family whose patriarch was stuck in the leprosy treatment facility for three months. We recall the Conference of Rulers parade we attended. Madame Ann also shows me a photo album filled with pictures of the refugee camp, as it was 45 years earlier when my family and I were residents. I'd become so accustomed to life over the course of the year I spent there that I no longer comprehended how poor the conditions were. I remember it being difficult, sure, but my memory has distorted a bit over time.

In the end, my family and I made it out of there, and we've all gone on to enjoy lives of privilege in America for many years. However, the photos sharply remind me that, in fact, it was an extraordinary challenge to survive at the camp. The hovels we lived in were so small; the clothes we wore were so ragged.

Later, alongside Madame Ann, I set my eyes upon the place where my family and I spent more than 13 months in a refugee camp. It's changed dramatically. Back when I was there it was all jungle. Today, it is a fully developed part of the city of Kuching. The only thing I recognized was the river in the back of the camp where we used to bathe and swim.

I think about all that I've provided for my family in the United States since I was last in this area of Malaysia. I reflect on how my wife Diana has always been so supportive. She raised our children and tended to our home while I was out almost all the time, at the restaurant and the countless events I attended as a caterer, host, or guest of D.C. power players. I can't describe how grateful I am to Diana for all that she's done for us.

I think of my daughter, and the incredible way she honored me by naming her first son after me — sort of. I thought she was joking when she told me in the early days of her pregnancy that the boy she'd deliver would be named "Jones." But sure enough, when he was born, my son-in-law, Ryan, texted our family group chat that "Jones Wiley Guthrie" had arrived into the world. I hope my grandson doesn't have as much trouble explaining his name to other people as I did. (Alisa gave birth to my granddaughter Lyla, who I love for her constant smiles, in 2023.)

I think of my son and how he's been able to make so many choices, safely picking and choosing his friends, where he studied and what he does for work. That has been my gift to him and he's taken full advantage of it, turning into an amazing man with a promising future.

Then there's City Lights of China and, even more importantly, the two Meiwah restaurants. It was with Meiwah that I was able to build a business all my own, just like my father did, afforded the chance simply by taking up residence in the United States. I was so proud that for the last 35 years, my businesses have employed hundreds of people, most of them are refugees or immigrants.

My Meiwah partners and I decided to close the D.C. location in May 2019. We had a huge farewell party that so many noteworthy Washingtonians we counted as friends and customers attended, including our former Secretary of State, Hillary Clinton and her Deputy, Huma Abedin. But it was bittersweet. My partners and I felt like we were forced to take such a drastic action and shut down the restaurant because our landlord required an exorbitant rent increase. We didn't want to ultimately work for him instead of ourselves. With that said, it was his right to seek a revenue boost from his property, and fortunately

Meiwah lives on in Chevy Chase, where I still mix it up with customers — new and old, prolific politicians and the people they serve just the same. I am so touched that we still welcome so many loyal customers that have been enjoying my restaurants' food for more than three decades.

This is the best country in the world. There's no comparison in terms of level of convenience and, certainly, in terms of opportunity. Work hard toward your goals and you will achieve them here, it's as simple as that. We must maintain that status as the land of opportunity, no matter the political atmosphere, and we'll continue to do so with the help of refugees like me.

There's a poster that I once saw hanging in the United Nations High Commissioner for Refugees' Washington D.C. office, in Dupont Circle, close to the original City Lights of China. The poster features an image of Albert Einstein. I mentioned it in the speech I gave after receiving the Outstanding Americans By Choice award. Addressing the 100 newly sworn-in citizens also in attendance, I said:

*Each and every one of you could contribute to our new country like Einstein did. Each of you has begun to live and experience the American dream. Yours is an exceptional opportunity not found anywhere else in the world to be measured by your own deeds and accomplishments. Learn, work, and participate in the processes of this country by learning and voting. Your lives and those you touch will be much richer for it.*

*All refugees and immigrants add their own section to the American tapestry. More than anything else, this tapestry has been woven by immigrants and refugees like all of us. Today's ceremony reminds me of that Einstein poster at the United Nations High Commissioner for Refugees office. It reads, "A bundle of belongings isn't the only thing a refugee brings to his new country. Einstein was a refugee."*

I may not have brought an extraordinary wealth of knowledge in the area of physics with me to the United States, but I'm proud to say I certainly provided this land with a few places to eat, talk, connect and smile. I'm so grateful to have had the freedom to do so, like every other American, from sea to shining sea.

*General Robert Magnus, Assistant Commandant of the Marine Corps*

*FBI Citizen. Academy graduation*

# SQUARE MOON

*Meiwah on TV, Lunar New Year feast*

*State of the Union Address 2013*

*Tim Cook, Apple CEO at the State Department*

*Amb. Capricia Marshall, Chief of Protocol with Diana and Alisa*

*ETSU Hall of Fame*

*Alejandro Mayorkas, León Rodríguez Outstanding ABC Award ceremony*

*Outstanding ABC Award Certificate*

*US Flag flown over the US Capitol 06-07-2016*

*50th Anniversary College Reunion 1974-2024*

*Saying farewell to Madame Ann 2024*

*Chief Sac Taupik Toh and family*

# SQUARE MOON

*The river was behind the refugee camp 2024*

*Hillary Clinton saying farewell to Meiwah DC 2019*

*UNHCR poster*

www.ingramcontent.com/pod-product-compliance
Lightning Source LLC
Chambersburg PA
CBHW040234110526
44582CB00002B/52